Principles of
The Counter Terrorism Process

A Guide for the New Guard of
Counter-Terrorism Professionals

David Gawel

Publisher: Inspiring Publishers,
P.O. Box 159, Calwell, ACT Australia 2905
Email: publishaspg@gmail.com
http://www.inspiringpublishers.com

A catalogue record for this
book is available from the
National Library of Australia

NATIONAL
LIBRARY
OF AUSTRALIA

National Library of Australia The Prepublication Data Service

Author: David Gawel
Title: Principles of the Counter Terrorism Process
          A Guide for the New Guard of Counter-Terrorism Professionals
Genre: Non-fiction

Paperback ISBN: 978-1-923087-97-2
ePub2 ISBN: 978-1-923087-96-5
PDF eBook ISBN: 978-1-923087-95-8

Foreword

This is one of the first times that a police officer who has stared terror in the face for a couple of decades, has written a "how-to" guide regarding understanding and fighting terrorism. His very personal experience in understanding, investigating and locking up those who have become radicalised seeps through every page.

Terrorism and its rapidly and dramatically evolving nature has made it essential for society to deal with the problem, to gain and maintain awareness of the issues, and to constantly develop solutions. As David quite rightly points out, in our society "all organisations now bear ownership of this threat." This book goes a long way to equipping organisations and individuals, in private and public sectors, with the 'tools' to deal with these often complex issues.

David's contribution to the narrative is extremely well timed and brings very real and valuable experience to bear. Three points make this contribution significant and unique. Firstly, David's extensive experience over decades in investigating terrorism, on the front lines of this threat; secondly, overlaying his decades in counter-terrorism operations are his many years in major and organised crime investigations and his deep understanding of law enforcement and its' community relations and policing; and thirdly, his academic achievement in pulling all these strands into a logical, structured construct to help people and organisations understand and deal with these problems, means he has a unique ability to apply contemporary knowledge and expertise to the issues.

This book provides practical steps, in a very contemporary context, to help with the four pillars of dealing with terrorism: Prevention, preparedness, response and recovery. But perhaps the work here on prevention and preparedness are the most significant, discussing means to introduce and improve understanding of how the threat originates and evolves, the identification of the threat, then focussing on the all-important decision-making process.

This focus is as innovative as it is enlightening. I found it to be extremely insightful, and I can see it being made compulsory reading for practitioners and professionals tasked with preparing organisations or studying in this space. It is an outstanding resource for those studying or training in all aspects of terrorism and its responses, as well as operational leaders who have a responsibility for the welfare of their staff.

To sum up, this book is a very valuable resource, with in-depth analysis, and a recommended balanced and nuanced construct to be applied by those operating in this space. It is written by someone who has spent his working life "where the rubber meets the road" and has academic rigour to his conclusions.

Nick Kaldas APM

Image:

Black swan: Nicholas Taleb in his book titled *The Black Swan: The Impact of the Highly Improbable,* identifies a theory he terms 'Black Swan'. The term is derived from the second century Latin expression that in summary stated that a black swan was rare because in essence it didn't exist. This phrase was based upon the flawed inductive reasoning where at that time all observed swans were white. In 1697 Dutch Navigator, William de Vlamingh arrived in Western Australia and discovered the existence of black swans (Cygus atratus), showing the impossible may later be disproven. Nicolas Taleb's Black Swan theory is a metaphor that describes an event that: is rare; has a high impact on society; but in retrospect could have been predicted. The parameters of such events appropriately apply to terrorist attacks. In this context the image of the black swan represents terrorism and terrorists.

Crown: The crown at the top of the sword symbolises legitimate governments that represent their people.

Sword: The word represents the conquering and destruction of a foe.

Meaning of the image: The people conqueror terrorism (counter-terrorism)

Contents

Part B: The Decision-Making Process

Introduction

The evolution of terrorism has expanded the responsibility for countering this threat beyond the remit of law enforcement and security intelligence to encompass all organisations within the public and private sectors. Counter-terrorism is now a joint government and community responsibility. This societal adjustment means that organisations that previously had no involvement now find themselves on the front lines of counter-terrorism. These new battle lines mean that those within these organisations who were traditionally not involved in terrorism have become counter-terrorism professionals within their specific fields of expertise.

This societal adjustment means all organisations now bear ownership in this threat. In other words, we have become the 'new guard' of counter-terrorism. This ownership translates into organisations having to comply with: counter-terrorism legislation; obligations of ensuring employee and customer safety; establishment of threat detection and reporting protocols; managing the increased risk of litigation; maintaining public safety and confidence; all whilst adhering to the community's expectations.

There is a void in instructional and reference material that addresses these new responsibilities. This book is primarily a 'how-to-guide' for organisations and their employees who are facing these challenges. This book achieves this by providing; practical tools and models that support organisations operational endeavours. It also provides reference material and the principles on counter-terrorism, which can enhance the development of effective policies and procedures that reduce the individual and organisations exposure to this risk.

The book provides practical solutions that cover the entire organisational spectrum from the practitioner up to the CEO[1]. In that, it offers easy-to-use tool boxes for practitioners or

---

[1] Chief Executive Officer

professionals and a critical decision framework that can be applied to all levels of management. The critical decision framework was developed and operationally tested to manage pressures and high stakes of the counter-terrorism environment. This framework has a secondary application, as it can be applied to any field where critical decisions are required to be made in a time-poor, fast-paced, high-stress environment.

The structure and content of this book means that it also is an excellent 'text' and 'reference' book for tertiary courses or any training in terrorism, security, threat and risk, critical decisions and criminology.

Terrorism in most jurisdictions is treated as a crime. This book will provide and explain the processes of counter-terrorism from the perspective of Western liberal democracy and the application of common law in an Australian context. In defining terrorism as a crime, it acknowledges that law enforcement and security intelligence are the lead agencies in combating terrorism. However, this approach accepts the new expanded ownership of this threat to the 'new guard' of non-traditional counter-terrorism organisations.

I am a preeminent counter-terrorism expert within Australia, having recently retired from the New South Wales Police Force (NSWPF) after 35 years of criminal investigations with my last 20 years specialising in counter-terrorism. I am Australia's most experienced counter-terrorism criminal investigator. I have conducted more than 2,000 criminal investigations into verified terrorist threats, which has resulted in preventing over three dozen terrorist attacks both in Australia and overseas. This exposure over the last two decades also means I have unfortunately borne a degree of ownership in the failings of half a dozen domestic terrorist attacks.

As a member of the Joint Counter Terrorism Team (JCTT), I obtained a Master of Arts and a Doctorate in counter-terrorism. These qualifications enhanced my operational research capabilities, so that I could maximise the lessons learnt from our previous mistakes and devise protocols that successfully combat terrorism. This operational research and establishment of new protocols resulted in numerous classified 'in-house' submissions, research papers and training packages that have altered the operating procedures for many government agencies.

I have held various strategic and policy roles for the NSW and Commonwealth governments. Some of these have included being a National Capability Advisor to the Australian and New Zealand Counter-Terrorism Committee (ANZCTC), the Director of the Counter-Terrorism Team, the Office for Police, NSW Government, a member of the NSW State Counter-Terrorism Committee, and the Manager of the NSW State Crisis Committee (for terrorism).

Thanks to these experiences, I can address these problems both theoretically and practically. Over the past two decades, I have dedicated my life to eradicating the threat of terrorism from our community. My experiences have enabled me to identify numerous effective principles and processes, providing practical solutions to the unique challenges encountered within this field.

The outcomes of a terrorist attack have far-reaching effects on the individual, their family, and the organisations involved. These impacts will be felt for years after the event. This was demonstrated from an Australian perspective following the Bali attacks in 2002 where 88 Australians were killed. This situation is intensified from an Israeli perspective when considering the aftermath of the Hamas incursion into Israel on 7 October 2023 where over 1300 innocent Israeli civilians were killed, sparking a conflict in Gaza. This book is based on the hard lessons learned from witnessing these events. My motivation for writing this book is to assist in preventing the recurrence of these tragic events by providing practical tools and models that can be applied in the real world.

Initially, this book will briefly examine the principles of counter-terrorism, then apply these principles through an overarching model referred to as the *Counter-Terrorism Process*. This is a three-part continuing model that will form the foundation of this book.

1

The Principles of Counter-Terrorism

1.1 Introduction

The principles of counter-terrorism as set out in this book are consistent, regardless of the motivation, strand of radicalisation, or extreme belief. In practical terms, this means these principles remain constant for all forms of religious, political and ideological terrorism. The purpose of examining these principles is to identify the potential challenges and opportunities when applying them in the counter-terrorism process. These principles, where appropriate, have been accompanied with case studies in order to assist a better understanding of their application.

1.2 Terrorism as a Crime

The foundation principle of this book is to treat terrorism as a crime and terrorists as criminals. This criminalisation provides the structure that enables society to prevent, manage, and recover. This book applies this principle through the application of common law from an Australian legal perspective.

Australia is a parliamentary democracy. It has a federal system of government (Commonwealth) under which the powers of the states are deferred. Australia also has one national definition for terrorism. It is based on the definition of a *terrorist act* as found in Section 100.1 of the *Criminal Code Act 1995* (Cth).

This section of the *Criminal Code Act* defines a *terrorist act* as an act or threat, intended to advance a political, ideological, or religious cause by coercing or intimidating an Australian or foreign government or the public, by causing serious harm to people or property, creating a serious risk to the health or safety of the public, disrupting trade, critical infrastructure, or electronic systems. It does not include lawful advocacy, protest, or industrial action.

Treating terrorism as a crime expands the responsibility of the organisations in the public and private sectors that now share the ownership of this threat. It also provides clear lanes of responsibility for each organisation that delineates the moving ownership of the terrorism threat.

1.3 Unique Crime

Terrorism as a crime has a number of factors that make it unique. These factors include its dynamic and protracted nature, existence of extremism, radicalisation, complexity, requirement for interoperability, international considerations, influence of government policy, scrutiny, impact on corporate reputation, and public safety. These and other factors require organisations to develop unique procedures for terrorism.

A common flaw is that organisations treat terrorism under the 'business as usual' model, thereby relying on standard procedures to manage and mitigate what may be a series of unique and significant events. An example of this principle is demonstrated in the following case study which depicts terrorism as a unique crime.

Case Study 1 – Unique Crime

Circumstances:

An employee of an organisation was the subject of an investigation by counter-terrorism authorities for attempting to travel to Syria to become a 'foreigner fighter' for the terrorist organisation *Islamic State*. The employee's management team were aware of the investigation and security concerns raised by the authorities. The management gave an undertaking to report any security issues they identified in relation to their employee.

After a couple of months, the behaviour of the employee began to change. He became argumentative with his colleagues and started adhering to a strict interpretation of his belief. He loudly espoused his beliefs and took periods of excessive sick leave.

Actions:

The behaviour of the employee, whilst a concern, did not constitute any offence or breach of the organisation's internal policies. It was determined that the employee did not pose any security concerns. As a result, the organisation didn't alert the authorities about the employee's changing behaviour. Instead, the employee was managed as per the organisation's standard operating procedure for excessive sick leave.

Independently, the authorities become aware of the employee's changing behaviour and amended their investigation plan. They commenced an investigation targeting the employee. This investigation established sufficient evidence to arrest and convict the employee, who was preparing to undertake a domestic terrorist attack. The significance of these unique behavioural changes was not recognised by the organisation, which treated him under the 'business as usual model', managing the employee as a poor performer (excessive sick leave). Fortunately, the authorities thwarted the intended terrorist attack. In this instance the organisation failed in its duty of care to report the actions of their employee to the authorities. As a result they would have held a degree of liability had the employee successfully undertaken his attack.

1.4 Victim-Based Crime

The primary purpose of terrorism is to influence others through fear. The application of this purpose manifests into creation of victims, since without victims there can be no fear or terror. In the counter-terrorism environment, the parameters for defining victims are considerably wider than those for traditional crimes. Here, victims can include the following:

- actual victims of the terrorist act
- perceived victims of the terrorist act
- targeted group of the terrorist act (including intended acts)
- families of these victims
- witnesses to the terrorist acts (traumatic incidents)
- families of the terrorists
- first responders
- counter-terrorism professionals

Due to this escalating wave of potential victims, these crimes require additional resources and the establishment of specialised protocols for the management and support of these additional victims. That is, the response to counter-terrorism should be a victim centric approach.

1.5 Other Crime Types

A tactic of terrorism is to create a mass casualty event with the aim to instil fear (terror) in the community. Whilst this might be the aim or result of a terrorist attack, not all mass casualty events are perpetrated by terrorists. Other types of crime also pose a significant threat and need to be either discounted or identified at such scenes. These other crime types include:

- grievance fuelled violence
- lone actors
- mental health
- fixated (non-terrorism)
- criminal

An example of other types of crime in a non-terrorism mass casualty event is described below in the case study on the Strathfield Massacre.

Case Study 2 – Mass Casualty Event (Strathfield Massacre)

Circumstances:

On Saturday, 17 August 1991, a 33-year-old unemployed taxi driver by the name of Wade Frankum (Frankum) was sitting in the Coffee Pot Café, Strathfield Plaza, Sydney. He was armed with a knife and an SKS 7.62 self-loading assault rifle. After four cups of coffee, he pulled out his knife and killed a young girl who was sitting in an adjoining booth. Frankum then commenced a 10-minute shooting spree through Strathfield Plaza. He fired approximately 50 rounds, killing seven innocent people, and wounding six more. When the police approached him, Frankum committed suicide by shooting himself.

Action:

During the inquest into these deaths, the NSW State Coroner, Mr. Kevin Waller found that Frankum's father had died of emphysema five years before

---

the massacre, and that his grief-stricken mother had subsequently gassed herself to death. Dr. Milton found that Frankum was never diagnosed with a severe mental disorder and did not have a history of severe aggression. Dr. Milton proposed that anger, guilt, and conflict in having no money were the motivating forces behind Frankum's rampage. In today's parlance, this is referred to as grievance-fuelled violence by a lone actor, and quoted as an example of a non-terrorism mass casualty event.

1.6 Preventative Nature

Counter-terrorism by its very definition is supposed to be preventative. The counter-terrorism professional, in essence, is required to thwart the intentions of the terrorist before they can manifest into an attack. In other words, they have to prevent the crime before it occurs.

To achieve this outcome, it requires professionals to possess a skillset specialising in anticipation. It is proposed to examine the principles of *anticipation* in a following chapter. An example of the preventative nature of counter-terrorism is demonstrated in the following case study on Operation Castrum.

Case Study 3 – Preventative Nature (Operation Castrum)

Circumstances:

On 9 February 2015, the Joint Counter-Terrorism Team (JCTT), Sydney received information that two men, Omar Al-Kutobi and Mohammed Kiad, were communicating with their handler in Syria who was a member of the terrorist organisation, *Islamic State* (IS). The purpose of these communications was to convince Al-Kutobi and Kiad to conduct a terrorist act in western Sydney on behalf of IS. On receipt of this information, the JCTT commenced an investigation in order to prevent this attack. The following day, Al-Kutobi and Kiad were seen purchasing a large hunting-style knife. A short while later, an intercepted communication with their handler revealed that these men were about to commence their attack.

Action:

Before they could act, the JCTT with assistance from the NSWPF Tactical Operations Unit (TOU) surrounded their premises in the western Sydney suburb of Fairfield. Al-Kutobi and Kiad were arrested without incident. Whilst

5

police were positioning themselves by establishing a parameter around the stronghold, Kiad and Al-Kutobi were inside filming each other holding the recently purchased hunting knife and making what is commonly referred to as a martyrdom video. In the video Kiad said,

"God willing, God willing, we will avenge our brothers and sisters and mothers and fathers in the land of Caliphate. I swear to God, we will avenge Burma, Afghanistan, Caucasus, and Chechnya and all Muslim lands.... I swear to God Almighty, yellow people, there is no reproach between us, you will only get from us the stabbing of your kidneys...."

At the scene, the JCTT members located an overwhelming body of evidence against the two men. The authorities believed that Kiad and Al-Kutobi were only 1 to 2 hours away from conducting their terrorist attack before they were prevented by the JCTT. On 9 December 2016, both men appeared before the NSW Supreme Court and were sentenced to 20 years' imprisonment.[2]

1.7 Community Expectations

Terrorism is a man-made event. This means from a community expectation perspective, all terrorist attacks are theoretically preventable. However, in the real world, this expectation is impossible to achieve due to an infinite number of factors. This expectation causes the community and governments to place unrealistic burdens on their counter-terrorism professionals. A factor for these unrealistic expectations is the community's expectation that reverses the responsibility for terrorism.

Frequently, in the aftermath of a terrorist attack, the community, at times driven by the media and politicians, the responsibility of an attack can be diverted away from the perpetrators and directed towards counter-terrorism professionals. This reversed responsibility can be attributed to the community holding these professionals to a higher standard. If they fail to prevent an attack, they may on occasion be considered responsible for its occurrence. Whilst this also occurs in other areas and industries, it is more prevalent in counter-terrorism. This reversed responsibility may manifest itself after a terrorist attack in some form of review by a

---

[2] CDPP

royal commission or tribunal, established to identify the perceived failures.

Another factor is community bias. The community has zero appetite for terrorism; the expectation is that it will not happen. History dictates that this is an aspirational expectation. Terrorism, as defined in the *Criminal Code Act 1995*, (Cth), has been present within Australia since 1801 when Governor King uncovered Australia's first terrorist plot by the radical Catholic Irish Fenians.

This zero appetite creates a community bias that does not reflect the true nature of the threat. Regardless of community expectations, terrorism, like all other crimes, is inevitable. An example of the consequences of the community's expectations is illustrated in the following case study, which highlights the scale and extent of measures undertaken by the NSW State Coroner and his team to conduct the coronial inquest into the Lindt café siege, which was identified as a terrorist attack.

Case Study 4 – Community Expectations
(Coronial Inquest into Lindt Café Siege)

Circumstances:

At 9:41 a.m. on 15 December 2014, an armed gunman entered the Lindt Café in Martin Place, Sydney, and took 10 customers and 8 staff hostage. He commenced a 16-hour siege with police that resulted in the deaths of two innocent victims and the gunman himself. As a result of these deaths, the NSW State Coroner ordered an inquest with two principal tasks:

- to investigate the circumstances surrounding the deaths of Tori Johnson, Katrina Dawson, and Man Haron Monis, and
- examine the actions of the police and authorities before and during the siege in order to assess whether they could be improved.

Action:

On 29 January 2015, just six weeks after the siege, the State Coroner commenced the inquest, taking the unprecedented step of broadcasting the opening remarks live on national television. In his final report the NSW Coroner stated that the reasons for this unprecedented broadcast was that,

"...it was imperative that the public component of the inquest begin as soon as possible to reassure the community that the terrible events of 15

and 16 December 2014 were being given the attention and scrutiny they deserve."

The investigation for the coronial inquest was identified as the largest critical incident investigation in Australia's history. It encompassed 1200 witness statements and 200 hours of media footage. A total of 14,690 witnesses were canvassed and 20 NSWPF officers were deemed as 'involved officers'. There was a review of over 1,000 hours of CCTV footage,172 emergency '000' calls, 1500 National Security Hotline calls, and 1712 calls from public information line. Over 10,000 running sheets were generated, 24,000 emails were received by the solicitor assisting the Coroner, and 132 witnesses were called to give evidence. There were 110 court sitting days resulting in over 8,000 pages of transcript,118 journalists registering to attend the proceedings, and over 68,000 pages in the brief of evidence. There were 32 organisations identified as being involved in the incident. All of this resulted in 44 recommendations being made.[3]

During the same year, the NSW Coroners conducted approximately 145 other inquests,[4] which by comparison were conducted with far less community expectations and scrutiny.

- The statistics quoted from the inquest are the result of the extraordinary efforts of the Crown, the investigative team and analysts.

1.8 Terrorism as an infinite Problem

Problem solving is a process where the problem is defined, circumstances are examined, and solutions are identified and implemented. A problem may have defined parameters, which is known as a finite problem. In contrast, a problem with no identified parameters is an infinite problem, and thus never-ending. This concept has been adopted from Simon Sinek's book '*The Infinite Game'*.

Traditionally, crime has been treated as a series of finite problems with clear parameters during its different stages. For instance, a crime is solved when the offender is arrested. Criminal proceedings cease when the jury gives the verdict at the end of the trial. The individual ceases to be a prisoner once they have completed their sentence. Once the prisoner has served their sentence and been

---

[3] NSW State Coroner (2017)
[4] H. Dillion (2019)

released from custody, they are considered to no longer be part of the criminal justice process unless, of course, they offend again. If so, a new problem commences and these processes are repeated.

However, terrorism unlike traditional crime is considered to be an infinite problem. Once an individual is identified as posing a potential terrorist threat, regardless of the stage of the treatment, the threat will remain indefinitely. This infinite threat becomes what is termed 'residual'[5] or 'enduring' threat. Instead of the traditional approach of solving crime, the management of this infinite threat is referred to as the management continuum.

Management continuum is the collective term for the perpetual treatment, mitigation, and resolution strategies implemented to address this infinite threat. The management continuum for this infinite problem is illustrated through the life cycle of a radicalised extremist in the diagram below:

Diagram 1.1:

THE MANAGEMENT CONTINUUM OF THE LIFE CYCLE OF A RADICALISED EXTREMIST

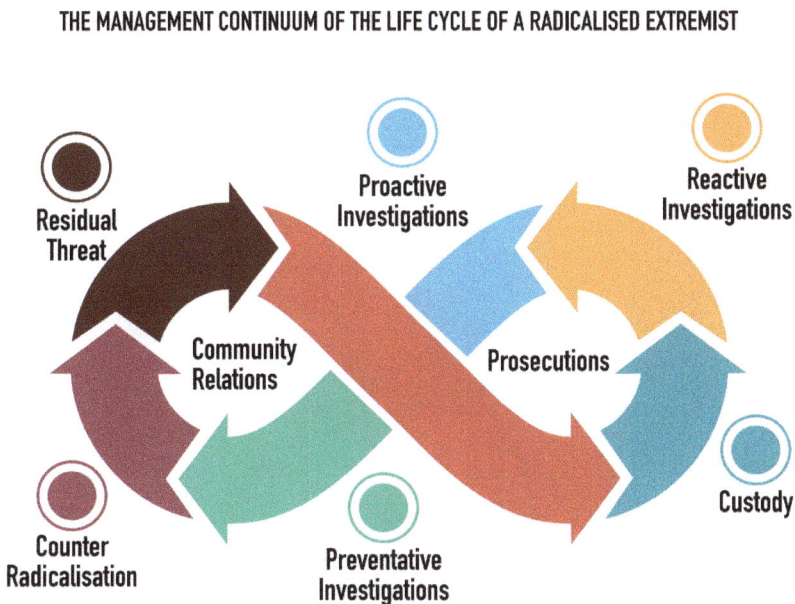

---

[5] Each agency, department, or organisation has their own term for residual threat/risk. It may also be referred to as enduring risk.

An example of infinite threat, which manifests itself into what is termed residual (enduring) threat, is demonstrated in the following case study.

> ### Case Study 5 – Enduring Threat (Khayre)
>
> Circumstances:
>
> In August 2009, JCTT Operation Neath foiled an Al Shabab terrorist plot to attack the Holsworthy Army Barracks in Sydney. The Melbourne counter-terrorism team in conjunction with their NSW colleagues, disrupted a mass-shooting plot that was in its early stages of planning. Five men were charged and placed on remand. The subsequent criminal trial saw three offenders convicted of terrorism offences and two alleged suspects acquitted. Yacqub Khayre (Khayre), was one of the alleged suspects found to have no case to answer and was acquitted of these offences.[6]
>
> On his release from custody, Khayre embraced his previous lifestyle of drug abuse and criminality. He continued his path of drug addiction and violent crimes, which included over 40 offences of burglary, theft, assault, drug possession, and firearm offences.
>
> Due to his extensive criminal history and lack of any evidence of his support for an extreme ideology, Khayre was considered not to pose a terrorism threat. As a result, he was no longer considered to be a national security threat and was managed as a suburban habitual criminal by local police. Given the known facts at the time, this was a reasonable assessment.
>
> His violent tendencies were demonstrated when, whilst on bail for an earlier malicious wounding, he was arrested and charged with committing a violent home invasion. When being sentenced for this home invasion, Judge Felicity Hampel stated that he was a young man with a "very sorry criminal record".[7]
>
> Unknown to authorities, whilst he was compliant with his conditions on parole, Khayre had begun to re-radicalise.
>
> Terrorist Attack - Brighton:
>
> On 5 June 2017, eight years after his alleged previous attempted terrorist attack, Khayre entered the Buckingham Apartments in the Melbourne

---

[6] Zammit, A (2012)
[7] The Guardian (2017)

Bayside suburb of Brighton. There, he shot and killed the receptionist with a sawn-off shotgun. He took a sex worker hostage and a siege with police commenced. During the siege, Khayre telephoned the Channel 7 news room and stated, "This is for IS, this is for Al Qaeda."

In the evening, Khayre exited his room armed with his shotgun, and charged at police, wounding two officers. He was shot and killed in the exchange of gunfire. The attack by Khayre was subsequently identified as a terrorist attack.

1.9 Radicalisation

Radicalisation is the process by which a person's mindset is altered to the extent that they move beyond lawful acts of advocacy, protest, dissent, or industrial action to a point where they are prepared to engage in acts of terrorism or commit crimes identified as terrorism offences. Radicalisation is not unique to terrorism and has been identified in other crime types as well.[8] However, there are two key principles for radicalisation and terrorism. First, the radicalisation process is unique to the individual. Second, whilst not all criminals are radicalised, all terrorists are considered to be radicalised.

Previously, radicalisation has been approached as a one-dimensional phenomenon, a 'one size fits all'. However, in reality, it is a multi-dimensional phenomenon. This book adopts the concept of the *strands of radicalisation*. This concept identifies that there are different forms or 'strands' of radicalisation. Each strand presents differently and will have different pathways, indicators, and characteristics. This concept is essential in effectively anticipating and countering terrorism. It will be explored in greater detail in later chapters. The general concept of the radicalisation process is demonstrated in the following case study.

---

[8] Dawson, L.

Case Study 6 – Radicalisation Process - JCTT Operation Newport (Willy Brigitte)

Background:

Willy Brigitte was a French national born in 1968 on the Caribbean island of Guadeloupe. Guadeloupe is an overseas department of France. He was brought up with his family in a Christian/French structured society in the Caribbean. He moved to Paris to finish his last year of school. Prior to finishing his schooling, he left and joined the French Navy where he served for three years. In 1993, he left the Navy and unsuccessfully attempted a variety of occupations, which included a butcher, social worker, printer, teacher, storeman, and drug rehabilitation worker. It appears that Brigitte had not succeeded in any of these careers. During this period, he was married and was a functioning member of the French community. At some stage during these various occupations, Brigitte, who was considered to be educated and well read, started to explore Islam.

Radicalisation Pathway:

By 1998, Brigitte had fully embraced Islam, adhering to an extreme interpretation of the religion, and adopting the new Islamic name of Mohammed Abderrahman. He began attending mosques known for their extremist views and links to Al Qaeda. He also started associating with known terrorists, attending prayer sessions and training camps. At some point in this progression, Brigitte became radicalised in that he was prepared to commit acts of violence and terrorism in support of his extreme interpretation of Islam.

Outcome:

- In 1998, Brigitte was arrested in Yemen for terrorism offences, being later released due to insufficient evidence.
- Whilst in custody in Yemen, he wrote a letter to his then wife stating that he wished to die for Allah.
- Members of his terrorist cell in Paris were linked to the assassination of the Afghan Commander of Northern Alliance, Ahmed Shah Massoud in 2001.
- After 9/11, Brigitte attempted to enter Afghanistan but was turned around in Pakistan.
- Subsequently, he attended numerous Lashkar-e-Taiba (LeT) terrorism training courses in Pakistan before returning to Paris.
- On 16 May 2003, LeT sent Brigitte to Australia to prepare for a terrorist attack.

- In October 2003, he was deported from Australia on immigration offences.
- On his return to Paris, Brigitte was investigated by the French counter-terrorism judge, Judge Jean-Louis Bruguière. Subsequently, he was charged with associating with criminals related to a terrorist enterprise, which included his intended terrorist activities in Australia. He was convicted at trial and sentenced to nine years in prison. He was released in 2009.
- Early in 2012, Brigitte was rearrested during a French operation of a suspected terrorist network.
- In September 2012, Brigitte left France bound for Syria, where he joined terrorist organisations — Al-Nusra Front, then Islamic State, and back to Al-Nusra Front.
- In 2017, it is suspected that Brigitte was killed during hostilities in Syria.

1.10 Terrorism: Risk vs. Threat

The concepts of 'threat' and 'risk' are two of the most frequently used concepts in the counter terrorism environment. Generally, they are relied upon as anticipatory tools for allocation and prioritisation of resources. Whilst these two concepts are separate, they complement each other in providing a complete picture of potential hazards.

Both threat and risk have separate and distinct roles, which means they are better suited to different situations. Frequently, they are misunderstood and mistakenly interchanged with one another. To assist counter-terrorism professionals and decision makers in effectively navigating these concepts, this book has adopted the following Terrorism Threat and Risk Principles.

Terrorism Threat and Risk Principle 1:	Risk is best applied to protecting the organisation, minimising the corporation's exposure to the dangers from terrorism. **RISK = Corporate Safety**

| Terrorism Threat and Risk Principle 2: | Threat is best applied to anticipating and protecting the community, minimising the public's exposure to the dangers from terrorism. **THREAT = Public Safety** |

Both principles are important in the counter-terrorism management continuum, which will be explored in greater detail in the following chapters. An example of the proposed application of the concepts of threat and risk in the counter-terrorism environment is given below.

Scenario 1 – Risk vs. Threat

Background:

A counter-terrorism team is managing multiple terrorist plots simultaneously. Each individual terrorism plot has multiple persons of interest (POI). Each plot is subject to individual investigations. The team prepares multiple risk assessments for each POI and terrorist plot. In Australia, the majority of government agencies and private sector organisations prepare these risk assessments by using risk ratings, which are calculated with the assistance of a threat and risk matrix. This can be a time-consuming and onerous process.

The team has limited resources and has to allocate these limited resources to the most appropriate individual POIs and/or plots. Each plot is fast-moving and the information is changing every hour. There is insufficient time to finalise the standard risk assessment without circumstances changing and requiring a renewed risk assessment.

Proposed Approach:

In such circumstances, when allocating limited resources in a time-poor, dynamic environment with focus on ensuring public safety, it is more effective to apply the concept of likelihood (i.e., threat) of the event occurring as a means to prioritise the investigations as opposed to determining risk. This issue will be explored in greater detail in the following chapters.

1.11 Small Datasets

Terrorist attacks are rare events in Western societies. The rarity of these events results in small datasets for examination and study of these crimes. In contrast to traditional (reactive) crimes such as, burglaries, assaults, malicious damage, stealing, which frequently occur. The high occurrence of these types of crimes allow for large datasets to be developed and the problem to be analysed with greater certainty. Statistics that support the challenges of examining small datasets is set out in the case study on small datasets for terrorism in Australia.

Case Study 7 - Small Datasets for Terrorism in Australia*

Percentage of convicted terrorists to Australia's Population: .00000385%

Percentage of NSW prison inmates that are terrorists: .00232%

Percentage of Australian deaths resulting from domestic terrorism: .000026%

*Statistics are approximate and based on available data as of 2022. BOCSAR and open source.

Examination of such small datasets may result in bias, over, or under-estimation of variance, and/or be imbalanced. These issues make the analysis of small datasets unreliable, which makes the development of consistent and reliable models more challenging.

1.12 Summary

The principles of counter-terrorism as set out in this book are consistent, regardless of the motivation, strand of radicalisation or extreme belief. In practical terms, this means these principles remain constant for all forms of religious, political and ideological terrorism.

The foundation principle for this guide is to treat terrorism as a crime and terrorists as criminals. This criminalisation provides the framework that enables society to prevent, manage, and recover. Treating terrorism as a crime expands the responsibility of the organisations in the public and private sectors that now share the ownership of this threat. It also provides clear lanes of responsibility for each organisation that delineates the moving ownership of the terrorism threat.

It is a common flaw in organisational procedures to treat terrorism under the 'business as usual' model, thereby relying on standard procedures to manage and mitigate what may be a series of unique and significant events.

Terrorism is a victim-based crime; whose primary purpose of terrorism is to influence others through fear. The application of this purpose manifests into creation of victims, since without victims there can be no fear or terror. The parameters for defining victims in this environment is considerably wider than those for traditional crimes. Hence it is recommended that counter-terrorism apply a victim centric approach. This book considers terrorism to be an infinite threat, that is once an individual is identified as posing a potential terrorist threat, regardless of the stage of the treatment, the threat will remain indefinitely. This infinite threat becomes what is termed 'residual' or 'enduring' threat. The perpetual treatment and management of this infinite threat is through the management continuum.

Radicalisation is a multi-dimensional phenomenon. This book adopts the concept of the *strands of radicalisation*. This concept identifies that there are different forms or 'strands' of radicalisation. Each strand presents differently and will have different pathways, indicators, and characteristics.

1.13 Key Points

- Terrorism is a rare man-made event.
- The principles of counter-terrorism remain constant.
- Terrorism is a crime and terrorists are criminals.
- Organisations in both public and private sectors bear the ownership of this crime.
- Terrorism is a unique victim-based crime.

- Counter-terrorism by its definition is preventative, however the expectation that all acts of terrorism are preventable is unrealistic.
- Terrorism is an infinite threat that is mitigated through the management continuum.
- This book identifies that there are different forms or 'strands' of radicalisation. Each strand presents differently and will have different pathways, indicators, and characteristics.
- The concepts of threat and risk have separate and distinct roles, which means they are better suited to different situations.

2

The Counter-Terrorism Process

2.1 Introduction

Counter-terrorism is a series of perpetual interrelated processes specific to each circumstance. The overarching structure is referred to as the counter-terrorism process. It is a three-part process through which terrorism threats can be effectively managed in both the public and private sectors.

This book will set out a formulated approach for organisations to adopt during each stage of the counter-terrorism process, in order to manage terrorist threats. The aim of the process is to maximise the efficiency of counter-terrorism activity whilst minimising the organisations' risk exposure to the threat.

The principles of counter-terrorism will be examined from the perspective of each of the components of the process. The counter-terrorism process comprises of three parts, which are structured as below:

1. Part A: Collection Process
2. Part B: Decision-Making Process
3. Management Continuum

An illustration of the counter-terrorism process is set out in diagram 1.1.

Diagram 2.1:

THE COUNTER TERRORISM PROCESS

PART A
The Collection
Process

PART B
The Decision
Making Process

Management Continuum

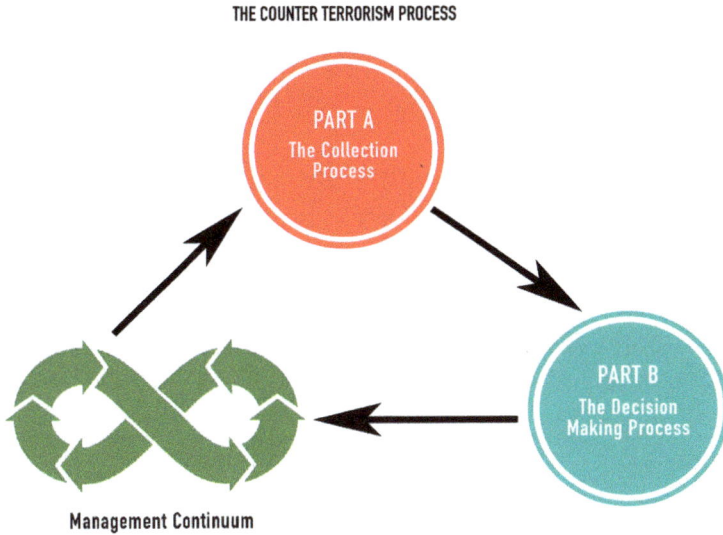

2.2 Part A: Collection Process

The *collection process* incorporates every activity undertaken by counter-terrorism professionals when gathering and/or assessing information on a terrorist threat. In the counter-terrorism environment, the greater the volume of collected material, the greater the capacity for preventing an attack.

Information gathering occurs through what this book refers to as *collection points*. A collection point is any action or interaction by or with a person of interest (POI) that potentially provides information on their intent. This collection of information is undertaken by the counter-terrorism capabilities.

Counter-terrorism (collection) capabilities are the various areas in public and private sectors that gather information from the collection points through their operational methodologies. Counter-terrorism capabilities can include intelligence, investigations, surveillance, prosecutions, custody, data mining, corporate holdings and case management.

The collected information is analysed and assessed. This assessment is then reported to the decision maker. Once this is done, the counter-terrorism process moves to the next phase, Part B: Decision-Making Process.

To summarise, the components in the collection process include:

- collection
- through collection points
- by counter-terrorism capabilities
- analysis of information
- report to the decision maker

An illustration setting out the collection process is given below in diagram 2.2.

Diagram 2.2

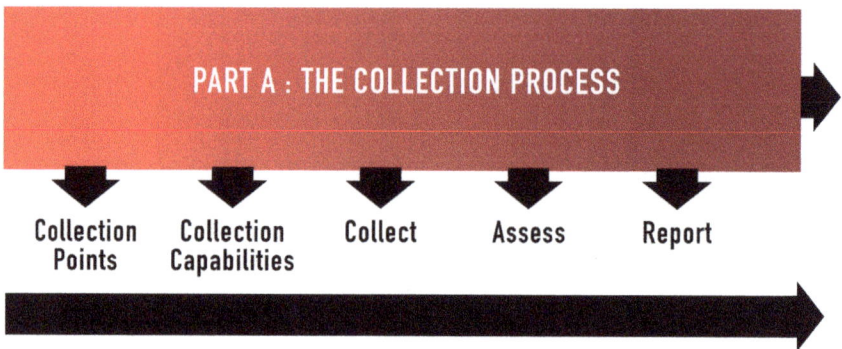

PART A : THE COLLECTION PROCESS

| Collection Points | Collection Capabilities | Collect | Assess | Report |

2.3 Part B: Decision-Making Process

Decision-making is a complex process that is unique to each decision maker and organisation. It commences when the decision maker receives the assessed information (report) from the collection process. It incorporates multiple steps that may occur simultaneously with each other.

The decision maker initially analyses the reported information from the collection process. This assessment is then used to anticipate potential future outcomes as well as cognitively evaluate the uncertainties to form an opinion or *judgement*. The decision maker then uses this judgement to decide on the best course of action, and takes action for the implementation of their *decision*. Ultimately, this process requires the decision maker to make the optimum choice from a series of alternatives, and then take action to *implement* that choice.

The components in the decision-making process briefly include:

- *assess* the context and significance of the information
- *anticipate* the possible outcomes
- cognitively evaluate the uncertainties to form a *judgement*
- make a choice (*decision*) on the best alternative based on judgement
- *implement* that choice

A diagram setting out the decision-making process is illustrated below.

Diagram 2.3

PART B : COUNTER TERRORISM PROCESS " DECISION MAKING PROCESS"

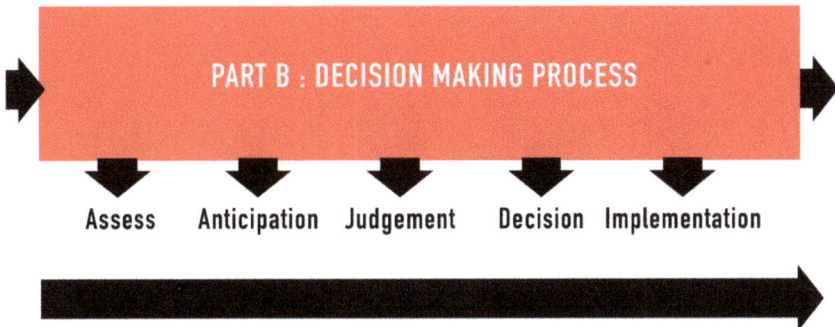

PART B : DECISION MAKING PROCESS

Assess   Anticipation   Judgement   Decision   Implementation

2.4 The Management Continuum

Management continuum is the collective term for all the strategies that are determined via the decision-making process and applied to managing a terrorist threat. These may incorporate treatment strategies, management strategies, mitigation strategies, and/ or resolution strategies. Once a terrorist threat is identified, it remains indefinitely; that is, it is an infinite problem.

The management continuum represents the perpetual decision-making process in response to a terrorism threat. This perpetual concept is represented in this book through the infinity symbol, which may represent any of the following strategies:

- deployment of collection capabilities
- threat/risk assessments
- commencement of preventative, proactive, or reactive investigations
- resolution
- prosecution
- custody
- any other interdiction strategies
- de-radicalisation (treatment)
- community relations
- engagement of other services (health, education, NGOs)
- residual threat protocols
- victim liaison
- no active collection activity

2.4.1 No Active Collection

No active collection is a deliberate decision to stop collecting information on an identified potential terrorist threat. This is a legitimate decision driven by the limited counter-terrorism resources that compete against an ever-increasing pool of potential terrorist threats. It aims to redirect limited counter-terrorism resources to another threat that is deemed to have a higher veracity. This is an unfortunate reality of competing priorities that impact the management of an infinite threat. It should be noted that the collective pool of persons of interest (POIs) deemed to be subject to *no active collection* globally pose the highest threat of terrorism. This concept is referred to as an *enduring threat*, which will be addressed in a later chapter.

A diagram setting out the concept of management continuum is illustrated below:

Diagram 2.4

THE MANAGEMENT CONTINUUM OF THE LIFE CYCLE OF A RADICALISED EXTREMIST

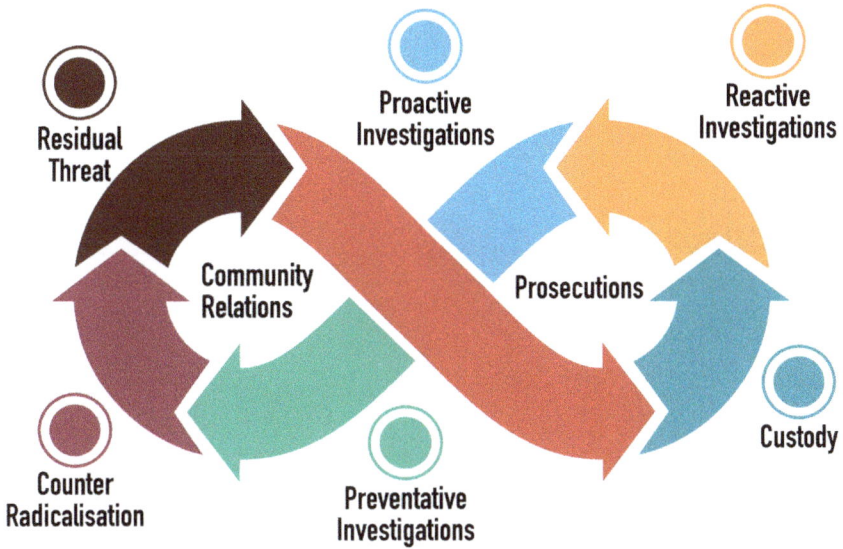

Residual
Threat

Proactive
Investigations

Reactive
Investigations

Community
Relations

Prosecutions

Counter
Radicalisation

Preventative
Investigations

Custody

PART A

THE COLLECTION PROCESS

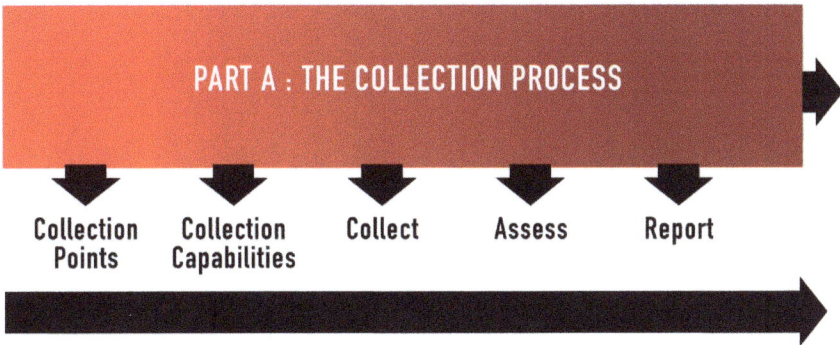

PART A : THE COLLECTION PROCESS

Collection Points | Collection Capabilities | Collect | Assess | Report

3

Counter-Terrorism Collection Capabilities

3.1 Introduction

In the context of terrorism, *collection* is any activity undertaken by counter-terrorism professionals in their course of business that is capable of gathering information. Every action or interaction by or with a person of interest (POI) that provides information on their intentions is a *collection point*. *Counter-terrorism capabilities* are the disciplines that collect the information from these collection points via their various collection techniques (methodology). The information obtained from collection points is assessed and reported to the decision maker(s) to facilitate the decision-making process.

The number of potential collection points in modern society is infinite: they may include interactions with the POIs during interviews, conversations, social media, meetings, associations, and engagements. These collection points may occur through dealings with the following areas: law enforcement, custody, legal, retail, transport, finance, entertainment, health, utilities, security, education, employment, social interactions and communications, to name a few.

Counter-terrorism collection capabilities are present in all organisations within the public or private sectors. Examples include managing databases, auditing, financial services, training, customer service, cyber activity, community engagement, enforcement, legal proceedings and general business activity.

From a law enforcement and security intelligence perspective, counter-terrorism capabilities in Australia and New Zealand are centrally coordinated through one agency, the Australian and New Zealand Counter Terrorism Committee (ANZCTC). In the context of this book, officers engaged in collection capabilities of either public or private sectors are considered as counter-terrorism professionals.

The purpose of these collection capabilities is to enhance the ability of the organisation in identifying, mitigating, managing, or preventing terrorist attacks via the management continuum. In the event that a terrorist attack has occurred, the purpose of these capabilities is to identify what occurred and who was responsible, so as to aid in the community's resilience and recovery.

3.2 Intelligence

Intelligence has numerous applications to a range of disciplines. In accordance with the principal concept of this book, the definition for intelligence under this setting aligns itself to the criminal justice system. Intelligence is the process of value-adding to the information retrieved from collection points through examination and analysis. This may be achieved through an infinite number of processes, such as the 'intelligence cycle'. Generally, counter-terrorism intelligence professionals manage their collection via 'collection plans'.

Value-adding to the collected material leads to the creation of 'intelligence products'. Intelligence products include a wide range of materials in multiple formats. The nature and contents of intelligence products is determined by the intended end user or client of the products. Examples of these products may include alerts, briefing, assessments, situation reports, intelligence reports and analytical assessments, which may be supported by charts, diagrams and statistics graphs. These products are tailored to meet the needs of the various clients or end users of these products.

The primary client for these intelligence products will change in parallel with the ownership of the threat. This means different counter-terrorism capabilities will take priority at different stages as they assume principal ownership of the threat as it moves through the management continuum. An example of the role of intelligence is set out below in the case study – intelligence.

Case Study 8 – Intelligence (JCTT Operation Silves)

Background:

In 2017, the Joint Counter-Terrorism Team (JCTT) Sydney received information from a partner agency that two unknown males were planning to conduct a terrorist attack on behalf of the terrorist group *Islamic State* by placing a bomb on a commercial airliner with the intention of killing all of the passengers.

Management Continuum - Intelligence:

Initially, the intelligence unit within the JCTT was given the ownership of this threat and tasked to analyse the information in order to ascertain if it was a creditable threat and to identify the unknown persons of interest (POIs). This meant that the intelligence collection capability had the priority at this stage.

Management Continuum – Investigations:

Once the intelligence unit of JCTT had successfully identified the POIs and that it was a creditable threat, a decision was made via the management continuum to transfer the ownership of this threat to the investigators: they were tasked to investigate the information with a view to determining if criminal offences were being committed. As a result, the priority had now been transferred to the investigations collection capability and the intelligence capability was tasked with supporting the criminal investigation.

Management Continuum – Tactical Operations:

The investigations capability established that criminal offences had been committed and that there was sufficient evidence to warrant the arrest of the identified POIs. Given the circumstances and the fact that the POIs were identified as posing a terrorist threat, the decision was made to transfer the ownership of the threat during the arrest phase to the specialist tactical police capability (TOU). The intelligence capability was tasked with supporting and providing intelligence products that would support the tactical police in safely arresting the POIs.

Management Continuum - Investigations:

Once the tactical police arrested the POIs, the decision was made to transfer the ownership of the threat back to the investigations capability who were tasked to prepare a brief of evidence in order to criminally prosecute the POIs. The intelligence capability was tasked with providing intelligence products to support and be included in the brief of evidence against the POIs.

3.3 Investigations

Investigations in their simplest form are regarded as the processes of searching for facts. To align a definition with the principal concepts of this book, investigations are defined as determining the facts through collection of information. From the law enforcement perspective, this process is undertaken to a higher level in that the information is collected to an evidentiary standard for production in court. Due to this higher evidentiary standard, there is a reliance on investigations by the prosecution capability. This reliance has generally resulted in the investigations capability assuming responsibility and overall coordination of counter-terrorism operations.

In response to the evolving nature of terrorism, new disciplines in terrorism investigations have evolved to meet the demands of this changing environment. Thus, there are different types of terrorism investigations that differ in their purpose and timing in the lifecycle of the threat. The new investigative disciplines include preventative investigations, proactive investigations, and reactive investigations.

In general terms, these investigations reflect the escalating nature of the threat. Preventative investigations precede 'proactive investigations', which in turn precede 'reactive investigations'. This concept is set out below (Diagram 3.1: Terrorism Investigations Model).

Diagram 3.1: Terrorism Investigations Model

TERRORISM INVESTIGATIONS MODEL

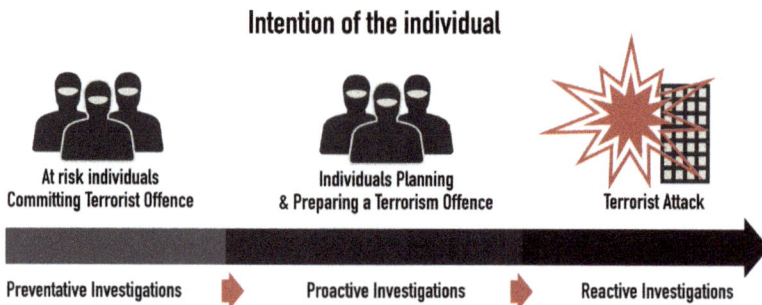

Intention of the individual

At risk individuals Committing Terrorist Offence

Individuals Planning & Preparing a Terrorism Offence

Terrorist Attack

Preventative Investigations → Proactive Investigations → Reactive Investigations

3.3.1 Preventative Investigations

Preventative investigations have recently evolved in order to address the enduring threat that is primarily posed by incarcerated POIs. These investigations are aimed at POIs who are considered to pose high risk in committing a terrorist offence but have not yet offended or reoffended. This refers to those POIs that are classified as being a 'residual or enduring threat'. The term 'residual threat' signifies the threat of terrorist attack being perpetrated by an offender that was previously assessed and/or has been of interest to authorities from a terrorism perspective but was considered at that time not to constitute a threat.

Each jurisdiction manages this phase of the threat differently. Preventative investigations include those investigative activities that mitigate actual or perceived terrorist threats. In so doing, support counter-radication and de-radicalisation functions, such as targeted engagement and support programs, community engagement, intervention, health/welfare, and post-sentence detention/supervision schemes. Colloquially, this may be considered a preventative treatment approach in managing the threat.

In Australia, these investigations support: counter violent extremism (CVE) programs, engagement programs, community resilience programs, community corrections (parole), and activities covered under the *High-Risk Terrorism Offenders Act (Cth)* (HRTO) and *Terrorism High Risk Offenders Act* 2017 NSW (THRO). An example of a preventative investigation is set out below in the case study – preventative investigations (THRO):

Case Study 8 – Preventative Investigations (THRO)

Circumstances:

A corrections facility received information that one of their inmates who was in custody for robbery offences however was now a national security concern due to his associations and adherence to an extreme interpretation of his belief. It was also suspected that he was becoming radicalised. The corrections department believed that this inmate would pose a terrorism threat to the community on his release from prison.

Action:

The matter was referred to the preventative investigations team (for example in NSW, Terrorism High Risk Offenders Unit, THRO). The investigation established that the inmate had been associating with convicted terrorists whilst in custody. Further, the inmate had espoused support for the terrorist ideology and a willingness to continue supporting their violent ideology on his release from prison.

Whilst the inmate had not committed any criminal offences, he posed an unacceptable threat. The matter was referred to post-sentence/supervision schemes of that jurisdiction, in this case the THRO Team, in order to mitigate the threat via the management continuum.

3.3.2 Proactive Investigations

Proactive investigations commence when the POI's activity progresses and their intention is identified as potentially constituting a terrorism offence. These investigations involve investigating an intended crime and are based on the concept of 'pre-emption'. The aim of these investigations is to proactively avert an imminent act of terrorism. This is achieved by collecting evidence against the POI(s) to the point that a prima facie case is built.

Subsequently, this terrorism threat is eliminated by incarcerating the POI(s) with criminal offences before they can undertake their terrorist act. Driven by the necessity for it, the majority of liberal democratic societies throughout the world have adopted pre-emptive legislation to facilitate this category of investigation in relation to terrorism. An example of a proactive investigation is set out below in the case study – proactive investigations.

Case Study 9 – Proactive Investigations

Circumstances:

Police received information from the community that a POI who adheres to an extreme right wing (XRW) belief, intended to conduct a terrorist attack on behalf of their belief.

Action:

The matter is referred to the Joint Counter-Terrorism Team (JCTT) who commenced a criminal investigation. They confirmed the POI adhered to an XRW belief and was planning and preparing to conduct a terrorist attack on an electrical power station. The investigators observed the POI conducting reconnaissance on the target: they captured evidence of the POI researching the target on the internet as well as researching bomb-making instructions. The POI also had access to firearms. Consequently, the investigation determined there was a prima facie case against the POI of preparing and planning to conduct a terrorist act. The POI was arrested and charged and incarcerated for preparing to conduct a terrorist attack. The incarceration of the POI eradicated the threat of that terrorist attack.

3.3.3 Reactive Investigations

A reactive investigation is conducted in response to a crime that has been committed, such as a terrorist act or mass casualty event. This includes investigations into mass casualty events committed by non-terrorism crime types. Reactive investigations are the most frequent types of investigation undertaken by investigators outside of the terrorism environment.

The emergency response to a terrorist act from an investigative perspective is a reactive investigation. Reactive investigations also fall under 'Emergency Management' protocols. Each jurisdiction will manage their emergency response and subsequent reactive investigations differently. The investigative structure and remit for each reactive investigation will be determined by the nature and circumstances of the crime. Subsequent investigations, inquiries, royal commissions, or reviews into the response by authorities to a terrorist attack (reverse responsibility) and cold case investigations also fall within this category. An example of a reactive investigation is set out below in the case study – reactive investigations (JCTT Operation Peqin/Fellows):

Case Study 10 – Reactive Investigations (JCTT Operation Peqin/Fellows)

Circumstances:

On 2 October 2015, a young person dressed in religious robes and armed with a handgun walked up to the front entrance of NSW Police Headquarters, Charles Street, Parramatta. The young person followed an unarmed civilian staff member as the latter left the building after finishing his work for the day. The young person walked up directly behind the innocent civilian, pulled out his gun, and shot and killed him. The young person then yelled, 'Allah Akbar!' and fired several shots at the entrance to NSW Police Headquarters. The young person was subsequently shot and killed by a Special Constable during an exchange of gun fire. The Special Constable's job was to protect the building and its occupants. A crime scene was established and specialist police were called to attend to and investigate the crime.

Action:

The incident was investigated as a 'critical incident' due to the young person being shot by a Special Constable of Police. During the investigation, the detectives located a martyrdom letter on the body of the young person. Further evidence was gathered during the investigation, indicating the young person's adherence to an extreme interpretation of Islam. The matter was later identified as an act of terrorism. In this instance, the investigation occurred in reaction to the crime being committed.

3.4 Cyber Operations

Organisations in both private and public sectors have recognised the vital role of cyber operations in the overall management strategies for their organisations. Cyber operations are a complex area that includes multiple disciplines such as monitoring, collection, analysis, and engagement via social media. It also includes protocols that protect an organisation's computer systems and servers from being hacked and denial-of-service attacks.

This hybrid collection capability primarily incorporates aspects of both intelligence and investigation as well as encompassing a wide range of activities and unique collection techniques for the online space. It is a critical capability in its own right whilst also supporting the other collection capabilities. An example of this capability is demonstrated below in the case study – cyber operations.

Case Study 11 – Cyber Operations (JCTT)

<u>Circumstances:</u>

A cyber operative, whilst scraping various social media platforms, identified a direct threat against a foreign Prime Minister who was about to undertake an official visit to Australia.

<u>Action:</u>

The cyber operative conducted numerous inquiries and identified the POI through his online footprint. The cyber operative commenced an online covert engagement strategy against the POI. This strategy captured online evidence to a prima facie standard against the POI in relation to him making threats against the foreign Prime Minister. The POI was arrested and convicted for his online threats. The foreign Prime Minister subsequently undertook his official visit to Australia without further incident.

3.5 Custody

Traditionally, the incarceration of an inmate was viewed as the final stage of the legal justice process (when viewed from a finite problem perspective). Little value was placed on the potential information collected on the POI in relation to their enduring threat to the community. Whilst it is acknowledged that the primary role of a correctional facility and its officers is to ensure the good management and safety of that facility, it also provides an opportunity for custody officers to collect information on inmates identified as terrorism POIs.

The timely reporting on these POIs to decision makers may assist in accurate assessments of the potential threat they may pose internally to the correctional facility and/or externally to the wider community. A number of strategies in the management continuum rely on the potential information sourced from custody facilities.

3.6 Counter-Radicalisation and Treatment

Counter-radicalisation refers to early intervention strategies aimed at preventing or inhibiting radicalisation in at risk POI(s).[9] These strategies are conducted with the support of preventative investigations and represent an emerging field in counter-terrorism, referred to as 'treatment'. The term treatment in this context refers to the mitigation and management of a POI who has been radicalised and/or is considered to be at risk of being radicalised.

Counter-radicalisation and treatment may include activities such as: targeted engagement and support programs, community engagement, intervention, counselling and post-sentence detention/supervision schemes. Generally, these activities are undertaken by health and welfare professionals.

The majority of these activities are conducted through a process known as case management. Case management is prevalent in the fields of health and social welfare. The interactions between the professionals and POIs provide collection points for assessing intentions of the POI. An example of this capability is provided below in the case study – treatment.

Case Study 12 – Treatment

Circumstances:

An individual, due to their personal circumstances and associations, was identified by authorities at being at risk of becoming radicalised. The individual was referred to a case manager within a government support agency. The individual was provided with counselling and financial support to assist in their management and treatment.

Action:

The individual's case officer noticed a dramatic change in the individual's behaviour, which caused concern. The individual's behaviour was reported to authorities whilst the case officer managed the individual and their behaviour,

---

[9] O'Reilly, J.

the potential threat of the individual was monitored by the authorities. In this instance, the individual's case officer was able to case manage the individual to a stage where the authorities were comfortable that individual no longer posed a security threat and the individual progressed to cease being considered a current threat.

3.7 Prosecutions

Managing terrorism as a crime from a finite-problem perspective has meant that the prosecution along with custody was viewed as one of the end phases of a counter-terrorism procedure. Consequently, the additional information collected during the prosecution stage, i.e., excluding the conviction and sentencing details of the POI(s), received little attention. Given terrorism is now treated as an infinite problem, prosecutions have evolved into another vital collection capability. An example of the information that can be obtained from this capability is provided below in the scenario – prosecutions.

Scenario 2 – Prosecutions (Op. Pendennis/Eden)

Circumstances:

A POI was arrested and charged with preparing to commit a terrorist attack under the auspices of JCTT Operation Pendennis. The POI pleaded not guilty and the matter was subjected to a contested trial. The POI was convicted by a jury of his peers and he was sentenced.

Results:

During the trial and sentencing, the prosecution collected an array of information in relation to the POI, which may assist future threat assessments of the POI. This collection identified information on:

- Family structure and their influence on the POI in relation to their offending;
- Early childhood experiences and history;
- History of associates;
- Associates and behaviour when in custody;
- Details of previous criminal convictions;
- Evidence of their radicalisation and extreme ideology;

- Psychological assessments; and
- POI's own comments and position on issues when subject to assessments by various experts and health professionals[10].

3.8 Family Liaison and Victim Support

Family liaison and victim support processes are well established within traditional crime types such as homicide and sexual assaults. However, within counter-terrorism, these processes are still in their infancy. Their primary purpose is to support these various cohorts either during or after a crisis. In addition to serving a supportive function, they also offer opportunities to ethically collect timely and vital information that may assist in determining the most appropriate course of action. This book recommends a victim centric approach to counter-terrorism.

3.9 Others

There are numerous other collection capabilities, most of which are undertaken by government authorities. These include security intelligence; physical and electronic surveillance; technical coverage; and tactical, ballistic, and explosive examinations.

These capabilities rely on transactional processes specific to each capability. From the perspective of law enforcement security intelligence, these processes relate to their collection techniques (methodologies). These methodologies are protected by common law under the auspices of public interest immunity (PII) and will not be explored in further detail.

3.10 Business Activity

Counter-terrorism is a whole-of-government and community responsibility. Every organisation in either the private or public sector carries out a business activity particular to that organisation. Regardless of the organisation conducting them, all business

---

[10] This relates to information which is served on the courts and becomes public record.

activities collect information. This information, no matter how remote it may seem, needs to be considered by counter-terrorism professionals when managing a threat. The more extensive the collection, the greater the likelihood of preventing a terrorist attack.

3.11 Golden Rule

Counter-terrorism collection capabilities operate in the shallow pool of the management continuum. This means these capabilities frequently overlap. These overlaps can cause confusion and adversely impact an organisation's capabilities.

To address this situation, there is a *golden rule* which all counter-terrorism professionals must adhere to in order to avoid potential failings. The golden rule is simple: each capability or organisation involved in counter-terrorism must '*stay in their lane*'.

This golden rule relies on the condition that each organisation has identified areas of responsibility, and these areas of responsibility are managed by their respective specialists or experts from their collection capabilities. The success in any counter-terrorism activity is dependent upon these specialists or experts. Adherence to this simple yet effective rule ensures efficient interactions between capabilities and organisations.

3.12 Measuring Efficiency

Measuring the efficiency of counter-terrorism activities is often viewed as being problematic. This is primarily due to its preventative nature. Success leaves a limited footprint or tangibles in which to measure efficiency.

It is proposed that reviewing the collection points for each capability provides measurable results that can be used to assess the efficiency of that capability. These efficiency measurements can be supplemented by assessing the volume and value of information processed.

3.13 Summary

Counter-terrorism is a whole-of-government and community responsibility. Every organisation in either the private or public sector carries out a business activity particular to that organisation. Business activities, regardless of the organisation, collect information. All information needs to be considered by counter-terrorism professionals when managing a threat. The more extensive the collection, the greater the likelihood of preventing a terrorist attack.

The purpose of these collection capabilities is to enhance the organisation's ability to identify, mitigate, manage, or prevent terrorist attacks via the management continuum. In the event that a terrorist attack has occurred, the purpose of these capabilities is to identify what occurred and who was responsible, and to aid in the community's resilience and recovery.

Traditionally, the prosecution and incarceration of terrorists were seen as the final stages of the legal process and viewed as having little value in the collection process. However, in identifying terrorist as an *infinite problem,* the value and vital role of these capabilities in the collection process is now being recognised.

Another emerging field in collection capabilities is those captured under the banner of *treatment.* This includes disciplines of targeted engagement and support programs, community engagement, intervention, counselling, and post-sentence detention/supervision schemes. Generally, these activities are undertaken by health and welfare professionals. The interaction between these professionals and persons of interest provides a rich source of valuable information for decision makers.

Counter-terrorism collection capabilities operate in a shallow pool; to avoid crossing over into each other's path, this book recommends adhering to the golden rule: stay in your lane.

3.14 Key Points

- Collection is defined as any activity undertaken by counter-terrorism professionals in their course of business that is capable of gathering information.
- A collection point is every action or interaction by or with a person of interest (POI) that potentially provides information on their intentions.
- Counter-terrorism (collection) capabilities are the disciplines that collect the information from these collection points via their collection techniques (methodology).
- Intelligence is the process of value-adding to the information retrieved from collection points through examination and analysis.
- Investigations are defined as determining the facts through collection of information.
- Due to the evolving nature of terrorism, new disciplines in terrorism investigations have evolved to meet the demands of this changing environment. These new disciplines include:
  - o Preventative investigations
  - o Proactive investigations
  - o Reactive investigations
- Proactive investigations are the most common type of investigation in the counter-terrorism environment. Reactive investigations are the most common type of investigation conducted by investigators outside the terrorism environment.
- Counter-radicalisation refers to early intervention strategies aimed at preventing or inhibiting radicalisation in at-risk POI(s).[11]
- Golden rule: Each collection capability or agency must 'stay in their own lane'.

---

[11] O'Reilly, J.

4

Language

4.1 Introduction

Communication is the transfer of information; this transfer is usually accomplished by the effective use of language. In the counter-terrorism environment, communication has two main aspects in which practitioners should be proficient. The first is internal language, which encompasses proficient use of language to communicate with colleagues, decision-makers, and other stakeholders. The second is external language, encompassing proficient use of language to communicate with those external to the organisation, such as government agencies, external organisations, the general community, and various sub-groups within the community.

Effective communication is a difficult balance to achieve. Internally, inefficient language may lead to misunderstandings and operational failings. Externally, it may unintentionally cause offence to sections of the community, result in a loss of confidence, or incite support for terrorism.

4.2 Internal Communications

Counter-terrorism professionals operate in a high-stress, time-critical environment. The ability of decision-makers to make sound judgements and good decisions in this environment is dependent on accurate and timely information. These professionals need to be effective at both receiving and transferring information. One aspect of this process is efficient vertical communication. Vertical communication is the process of transferring information upwards and downwards in a hierarchical structure. Practically, this necessitates the practitioner to brief up to their decision-makers. It also means managers need to effectively brief down to their practitioners.

Another aspect of internal communication is horizontal. Horizontal communication is the transfer of information among peers at the same hierarchical level. Practically, this involves the transfer of information among colleagues who are engaged in the different collection capabilities and/or organisations.

4.3 Internal Language

Internal communications require discipline in applying a standardised lexicon that is transferred along the agreed communication pathways. One of the main barriers to communication in the counter-terrorism environment is a deviation from these agreed-upon pathways during a crisis. Failure to adhere to the agreed communication pathways can be problematic and generally originates from a lack of discipline. Examples of failure to follow the agreed communication pathways are demonstrated in the following scenario and case study – communication pathways.

Scenario 3 – Communication Pathways

Circumstances:

Each state in Australia has its own unique response to a terrorist attack. These responses can be complex due to the competing priorities of the states and the Commonwealth. Generally speaking, the state is responsible for public safety and the deployment of state emergency first responders to the incident. The Commonwealth is responsible for supporting the state with Commonwealth resources, coordinating a pan-Australian response, and managing national and international implications.

These responses are intricate; there is an enormous amount of crossover between state and Commonwealth agencies. To ensure effective and timely communication across both state and Commonwealth governments during a crisis, communication pathways — that is, who is to be briefed and the hierarchy of those briefings — are jointly developed by the state and Commonwealth agencies and adopted as policy. In preparation, these pathways are practiced and rehearsed, creating an expectation that they will be adhered to when required.

Issues:

During a response to a terrorist attack, there is a tremendous need for information by all levels of both the public and private sectors. If, during a crisis, in response to pressure, loss of nerve, or failure to adhere to policy, an organisation briefs out of the agreed pathways or timings, it can lead to organisations and/or vital areas being bypassed and excluded from the information. This exclusion of information can result in false reporting and false assumptions. These communication failures can lead to poor decisions and an adverse impact on operational response, potentially causing governmental and/or organisational embarrassment.

Case Study 13 – Communication Pathways

An Australian counter-terrorism agency was conducting a proactive investigation which identified an imminent threat of an attack. During the course of this investigation, the information was frequently changing due to the volume of information and evolving circumstances. During this period, a counter-terrorism practitioner received what they perceived as vital information. (This information later turned out to be false). Instead of following the agreed pathways — that is, the information was to be sent through the Joint Counter-Terrorism Team (JCTT) where it would be analysed, assessed against all holdings and, when verified, it would be forwarded to all agencies simultaneously — in this instance, the practitioner decided to forward the information directly to their agency's executive, bypassing the agreed pathway within the JCTT and partner agencies. The executive of this agency then independently made numerous operational and strategic decisions that were contrary to the known facts at the JCTT.

This decision to bypass the agreed pathway caused confusion and a delay in the deployment of critical resources. It soon came to light that the agency had made these decisions based on incorrect information. Whilst this set of circumstances was professionally embarrassing for that agency, the situation was resolved, and the matter was successfully concluded.

To assist in internal communications, a standardised terrorism lexicon should be a basic principle established by every organisation engaged in counter-terrorism. In order for a lexicon to work, it must be clear and precise. It also needs to be complementary and understood by partner agencies or organisations. To assist on this matter, this guide has established a lexicon radicalisation toolbox, which can be used as a basis by an organisation to construct its own lexicon that addresses its specific needs.

4.4 Lexicon – Radicalisation Toolbox

The definitions set out below are the basis of the concept developed for this book, termed *Strands of Radicalisation*. This concept will be elaborated in a later chapter. The terms below outline the escalation of radicalisation by identifying stages in the progression. These definitions can be utilised by counter-terrorism professionals in identifying or determining the threat a POI may pose, from a terrorism perspective[12].

These terms are designed to be generic and cover any potential motivation of terrorism whilst depriving any perceived legitimacy in that motivation or belief. To assist in the practical application of these definitions they are set out below in Figure 4.1 in an easy-to-use toolbox:

Figure 4.1: Lexicon (Radicalisation) Toolbox

Term	Definition
Belief	The term *belief* includes any religious, political, or ideological convictions of an individual or group.

Term	Definition
Fundamentalist	The term *fundamentalist* refers to any individual that complies with the laws of that jurisdiction whilst holding a strict and literal adherence to a set of basic principles or adheres to a traditional form of belief.

---

[12] O'Reilly, J.

45

Term	Definition
Extremism	The term *extremism* in a terrorism context refers to a belief system that passively supports the advancement of a political, religious, or ideological cause through threats or actions as defined as a terrorist act under that jurisdiction's legislation. Further, that their belief system is no longer in line within the acceptable standards of that jurisdictions as determined by applying the 'reasonable person test'.

Term	Definition
Radicalisation	The term *radicalisation* in the context of terrorism refers to the process that causes the individual or group to be prepared, directly or indirectly, to undertake or threaten to undertake any act that is defined as a terrorism act under that jurisdiction's legislation.

Term	Definition
Counter-Radicalisation	*Counter-radicalisation* refers to an early intervention strategy, system or process, aimed at preventing or inhibiting radicalisation before it occurs.

Term	Definition
De-Radicalisation	*De-radicalisation* refers to an intervention strategy, system, or process aimed at persuading a radicalised person or group to modify their belief system to the extent that they do not contravene the definition of terrorism under that jurisdiction's legislation.

Term	Definition
Reasonable Person Test	The *reasonable person test* is a legal term, which in this context means, 'a person who possesses the faculty of reason and engages in conduct in accordance with community standards'.[13]

4.5 Explanatory Notes

4.5.1 Belief

The term *belief* includes all beliefs which may make an individual susceptible to radicalisation. This potential list of beliefs will evolve and develop over time in line with changed values in society.

4.5.2 Fundamentalist

Applying this definition means that a fundamentalist does not contradict any laws and adheres to the accepted parameters of that jurisdiction.

4.5.3 Extremism

In applying this definition, the individual has not yet committed a terrorism offence but supports the use of violence to further their belief. The standard applied is that, if the belief supports criminal/terrorist activity then it is considered extreme as it is against the lawfully accepted parameters of the jurisdiction.

4.5.4 Radicalisation

A radicalised person is someone prepared to commit an act that is defined as terrorism. In the context of this book, a radicalised person is a terrorist.

---

[13] Butt, P., Aitken, J.

4.5.5 Counter-Radicalisation

The aim of counter-radicalisation is to deter an individual or group from being radicalised before the process commences.[14] The ideal methods for counter-radicalisation avoid community alienation and encourage community cohesion whilst enhancing community-policing ideals.

4.5.6 De-Radicalisation

Once an individual or group has been radicalised, it is argued that they need to be de-radicalised. It is the aim of de-radicalisation programs to reduce the threat by encouraging these individuals to abandon their desire to undertake acts of terrorism and assist in their re-integration into mainstream society.[15] De-radicalisation (& counter-radicalisation) now incorporates an emerging field of *treatment*. The term treatment in this context refers to the mitigation and management of a POI who is at risk of being or becoming radicalised.

A practical application of these terms is set out below in the case study – language (radicalisation lexicon)

Case Study 14 – Language (Radicalisation Lexicon)

Fundamentalist

A practicing person of the Catholic faith who strictly adheres to the teachings contained within the *Book of Exodus* or literately follows the Bible to the letter, may be referred to as a Catholic fundamentalist.

Extremist

An individual who supports the ideology of Osama Bin Laden and the actions of Al Qaeda (AQ), their attacks of 9-11, and the killing of innocent victims. However, they offer no physical or financial support or engage in any activity that may further that belief. This individual may be referred to as an Islamic extremist.

---

[14] Pickering, S., Wright-Neville, D., McCulloch, J., Lentini, P.
[15] Neumann.

> **Radicalised**
>
> An individual who supports an extreme right-wing belief and is prepared to attack a minority or engage in an attack against a section of the community with a view to furthering their belief, may be referred to as a radicalised right-wing extremist or a terrorist.

4.6 Counter-Terrorism Parameters

The standardisation of terms contained within the above toolbox provides a language that is clear and precise. This approach ensures that in a high-stress, time-critical environment, the use of this simple lexicon reduces any potential misunderstanding while communicating vertically to decision-makers and horizontally to other collection capabilities or organisations.

Applying this lexicon also provides the counter-terrorism professional with clear parameters within which they can operate without infringing on the rights of citizens. It identifies and defines what constitutes a legitimate threat to the community, setting their operational parameters while protecting the practitioner and/or organisation from breaching any civil rights. The relationship of these terms is set out in Diagram 4.1: Counter-Terrorism Parameters.

Diagram 4.1:

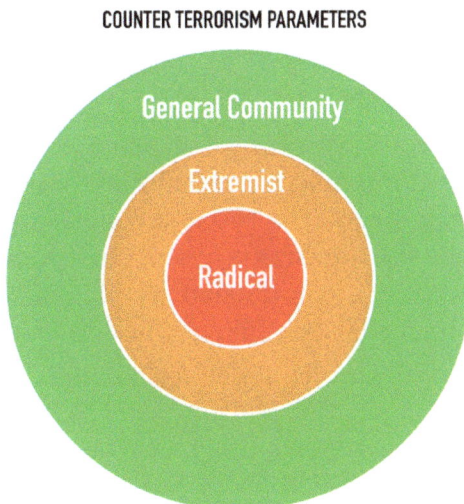

COUNTER TERRORISM PARAMETERS

General Community

Extremist

Radical

4.7 Acronyms

The use of acronyms is synonymous with communications within the counter-terrorism environment. An acronym is a word formed from the letters of other words that are frequently used in a specialised field[16]. The purpose of an acronym is to shorten the communication, making it more concise.

The main barrier to effective communications when using acronyms is being conversant with the meaning of the acronyms. Each collection capability, organisation, and level of decision-maker will have their own acronyms specific to their space. Further, the meanings of these acronyms evolve and change over time. Whilst the remedy for this communication barrier is simple, that is providing all parties with a list of their acronyms and meanings, this remedy is frequently overlooked by counter-terrorism professionals, especially during periods of high stress or when it is time-critical. Failure to communicate these simple meanings can lead to misunderstanding and confusion.

4.8 External Communications

The external audience for counter-terrorism professionals can include the general community, sections within that community, and organisations not engaged in counter-terrorism. The language used in these circumstances needs to be clear and concise in conveying the intended message. It is also vital to ensure that the language does not contain any perceived veiled messages.

There are generally two forms of external communications. The first is mass communications that may occur as a result of an organised event, or in response to a counter-terrorist activity. These messages are generally given by politicians and/or senior decision-makers, coordinated by their respective media departments or media liaison officers. Such communications may colloquially be referred to as 'public messaging'.

---

[16] *Concise Oxford Dictionary*

The practitioner's role in these instances, in conjunction with the organisation's media unit, is typically to prepare talking points, press conference briefings, formal written press releases or other forms of communications for release to the community via the media.

The second form of external communication is 'in person'. As it suggests, this involves communicating to individuals or groups either in person or via direct communication via phone, texts, emails or platforms such as FaceTime, Teams, Zoom, etc. This form of communication is undertaken by every counter-terrorism professional.

4.9 Veiled Language

Veiled language relates to either intentional or unintentional hidden meanings within language. These veiled meanings have occurred due to those adhering to an extreme belief corrupting certain aspects of a language or culture to suit their purposes.

The unintentional use of this veiled language to those aware of its alternative meaning may either offend and alienate sections of the community or encourage others by legitimatising their extreme beliefs. Examples of such language include using descriptive terms like, militants, soldiers, warriors, lions, operatives, mujahideen, freedom fighters, revolutionaries, guerrillas, commandos, assassins, martyr or martyrdom and insurgents to name a few. To address this issue, it is recommended that counter-terrorism professionals adhere to their organisation's agreed lexicon.

4.10 Summary

Counter-terrorism professionals operate in a high-stress, time-critical environment. Effective communication in this environment is a difficult balance to achieve. Internally, inefficient language may lead to misunderstanding and operational failings. Externally, it may unintentionally cause offence to sections of the community, result in loss of confidence, or incite others to support terrorism.

This book identifies essentially two broad forms of communication. The first is internal, which comprises vertical communication, incorporating the transferring of information upwards and downwards in a hierarchical structure. Horizontal communication involves the transfer of information among peers at the same hierarchical level.

Effective internal communications require discipline in applying a standardised lexicon that is transferred along the agreed communication pathways. This book has provided a lexicon toolbox, which apart from offering concise definitions, also provides counter-terrorism professionals with clear parameters within which they can operate without infringing on the rights of citizens.

The second form of communication is external, that is, communicating outside of the organisation or field. The language used in these circumstances needs to be clear and concise in conveying the intended message. It is also vital to ensure that the language does not contain any perceived veiled messages.

Acronyms are synonymous in this environment. Their purpose is to shorten the communication, making it more concise. However, the effectiveness of acronyms is lost if their meanings are not known by all parties involved. The success of any counter-terrorism activity is dependent on the appropriate use of language to effectively communicate the intended message in a timely manner.

4.11 Key Points

- The term 'belief' includes any religious, political, or ideological convictions of an individual or group.
- The term 'fundamentalist' refers to any individual that complies with the laws of that jurisdiction whilst holding a strict and literal adherence to a set of basic principles or adheres to a traditional form of belief.
- The term 'extremism' in a terrorism context refers to a belief system that passively supports the advancement

of a political, religious, or ideological cause through threats or actions as defined as a terrorist act under that jurisdiction's legislation.

- The term 'radicalisation' in the context of terrorism refers to the process that causes the individual or group to be prepared, directly or indirectly, to undertake or threaten to undertake any act that is defined as a terrorism act under that jurisdiction's legislation.
- 'Counter-radicalisation' refers to an early intervention strategy, system or process, aimed at preventing or inhibiting radicalisation before it occurs.
- 'Veiled language' relates to either intentional or unintentional hidden meanings within language.
- An 'acronym' is a word formed from the letters of other words that are frequently used in a specialised field[17].

---

[17] *Concise Oxford Dictionary*

5

Beliefs

5.1 Introduction

Belief is the fundamental component that delineates terrorism and extremism from other types of crime. These unique offences must be motivated by either religious, political, or ideological beliefs; otherwise, it is not terrorism. While religious and political motivations are generally self-evident, ideologically oriented beliefs can be complex and challenging for counter-terrorism professionals to define and label.

Instead of identifying the potentially infinite number of ideological beliefs motivating terrorism, this book proposes to classify them into three broad categories. This categorisation is based upon the generally accepted principles of these beliefs. It is acknowledged that there will always be a disparity in individual terrorist groups against the basic principles of the belief assigned to a category. It is also accepted that the belief system of each terrorist group will be unique and needs to be assessed on its own merit. However, the purpose of this generalisation is to aid counter-terrorism professionals in their assessment of these individuals and groups, as well as enhancing the decision-making process during the management continuum.

5.2 Beliefs

The term *belief* includes any religious, political, or ideological convictions of an individual or group and includes all beliefs that may make an individual susceptible to radicalisation. In a terrorism context, these beliefs form the foundation of the motivation that drives the individual or group to engage in terrorist activity. The list of beliefs that can potentially motivate terrorism is limitless. Further, this list continues to evolve over time, in line with the changing values in society. To manage this circumstance, this book proposes to group the potential ideological beliefs into three broad categories:

- Right Wing Extremism (XRW);
- Left Wing Extremism (XLW); and
- Issue Motivated Extremism (XIM).

5.3 Motivation

Belief is used by extremists to frame their motivation. Motivation is the internal force or desire driving the individual to engage in a behaviour. Whilst motivation has numerous forms, the two psychological forces of motivation to be dealt with here are 'intrinsic' and 'extrinsic'.

5.3.1 Extrinsic Motivation

Extrinsic motivation exists when the forces that drive the behaviour are external to the individual, including external factors such as punishments or rewards that influence the individual's behaviour. This concept is generally referred to as the 'carrot' or 'stick'. An example of this form of motivation is set out below in the case study — extrinsic motivation.

> **Case Study 15 – Extrinsic Motivation**
>
> Background:
>
> The offender is a convicted armed robber who has admitted that he commits his crimes for money. Police have received information that he is planning to commit another armed robbery on a local bank. Police speak with the offender and inform him that they are aware of his intentions and as a result, he is under police surveillance.
>
> Motivation:
>
> The offender does not want to be arrested and sent back to jail. The overt action by police has motivated the offender not to commit the armed robbery. This motivation, not to commit the armed robbery, came from the external force of punishment (stick).

5.3.2 Intrinsic Motivation

Intrinsic motivation exists when the forces that drive the behaviour are internal to the individual. This subjective process aligns itself with the identity and/or values of the individual. It is the identity and values that influence the individual's behaviour. Given that intrinsic motivation is intertwined with the individual's identity, it is seen as a more powerful motivator than extrinsic. An example of this form of motivation is set out below in the case study — intrinsic motivation.

> ### Case Study 16 – Intrinsic Motivation
>
> Background:
>
> The offender is a radicalised religious extremist, in other words, a terrorist. Police receive information that he is intending to commit a terrorist act. Police speak with him and inform him of their suspicions. He is informed that if he continues with his intentions, he will be arrested for terrorism.
>
> Motivation:
>
> The offender is motivated by his perceived religious obligation. Regardless of the prospect of imprisonment, he feels obliged to continue with his preparations to commit his terrorist attack, being motivated to commit the crime by his internal moral beliefs (intrinsic) despite being subject to the external force (extrinsic) of punishment.

The majority of criminal behaviour is motivated by extrinsic motivation; however, the majority of terrorism is motivated intrinsically. Intrinsic motivation is considered the more powerful form of motivation. This circumstance increases the complexity of preventing terrorism. It is also a significant consideration in the decision-making process during the management continuum.

5.4 Lexicon - Belief

The definitions set out below form the foundation for the three categories of ideological beliefs. They are not necessarily relevant or applicable outside this specific context. To assist in practical application, these definitions are set out below in Figure 5.1 in an easy-to-use toolbox:

Figure 5.1: Lexicon (Belief) Toolbox

Term	Definition
Belief	The term *belief* includes any religious, political, or ideological convictions of an individual or group.

Term	Definition
Extremism	The term *extremism* in a terrorism context refers to a belief system that passively supports the advancement of a political, religious, or ideological cause through threats or actions as defined as a terrorist act under that jurisdiction's legislation. Furthermore, their belief system is no longer in line with the acceptable standards of that jurisdiction as determined by applying the 'reasonable person test'.

Term	Definition
Right Wing Extremism (XRW)	XRW is defined as an extreme interpretation of either conservatism, authorism, nationalism, traditionalism, protectionism, or order.

Term	Definition
Left Wing Extremism (XLW)	XLW is defined as an extreme interpretation of either progress, equality, rights, or social environmental and animal welfare.

Term	Definition
Issue Motivated Extremism (XIM)	XIM is defined as an extreme interpretation of a predominantly single belief that is not considered religious, political, right wing, or left wing.

5.5 Characteristics

Each category of extreme belief presents characteristics that tend to be consistent. To assist in the practical application of identifying these characteristics, this book has prepared a toolbox for each belief below. These toolboxes catalogue these traits under the characteristics of motivation, leadership, and other general characteristics.

Figure 5.2: Characteristics (XRW) Toolbox

Categories	Characteristics
	XRW incorporates disciples from a broad church of hate. It includes neo-Nazis, neo-fascists, eco-fascists, protectionists, ethnic nationalists and so-called patriots. It transcends nations and cultures and is implicitly intertwined with its opposing extreme left-wing ideology (XLW).
Motivation	These groups are commonly motivated by conspiracy theories such as accelerationism, protectionism, anti-immigration theory, gender conspiracy and white genocide theory, to name a few. These theories motivate their members to act to protect an aspect of their identity, which they hold to be important. These conspiracies also support their narrative that they are serving a greater good for their cause.
Leadership / Structure	They tend to be centralised, hierarchical groups, characterised by their allegiance to an individual as their leader. Their membership predominantly consists of alienated misfits who, once they lose faith in their leader, will shift allegiance to another. This flaw causes these groups to have an unstable structure, which results in a cyclic process of XRW groups splintering into new groups.
	A number of these groups may view themselves as part of a wider international network; however, they tend to isolate themselves with like-minded individuals. This isolation makes them prone to groupthink.

	Like all forms of terrorism, XRW is influenced by world events, which may be aggravated by issues in their local environment. These groups are prone to 'copy' previous international XRW acts of terror. They hold terrorists who conducted successful attacks in high regard or as 'martyrs' for their belief.
Other General Characteristics	These groups support order and uniformity. There is a trend for them to adopt legitimate symbols and language, corrupting their meanings to communicate a unique aspect of their belief (veiled language). Due to their repugnant ideologies primarily based on hate, XRW groups can be subject to the incorrect bias that they pose a greater threat than other forms of extremism. XRW is mainly subject to generational, cognitive opening, fixated, and mental health radicalisation. This form of extremism may be perpetrated by groups or lone actors.

An example of this form of extreme right-wing belief is set out below in the case study — Nazi Bombing Brisbane Communist Party Headquarters (XRW).

Case Study 17 – Nazi Bombing Brisbane Communist Party Headquarters (XRW)

Background:

Extreme left –wing beliefs are in contradiction to the beliefs of neo-Nazi's and extreme right-wing beliefs. These differences propagate a cycle of perpetual violence between these two beliefs, right versus left and left versus right.

Details:

At 7.45pm on 19 April 1972, six sticks of gelignite exploded causing extensive damage to the Brisbane Communist Party Headquarters, Brisbane. Shortly after the explosion a male telephoned the news desk of the Courier-Mail newspaper and said:

"I am a member of a right-wing group. We have just bombed the Communist Party Headquarters in St Pauls Terrace. We will bomb more on Friday if they march in the moratorium. It is Hitler's birthday tomorrow. Heil Hitler."

At 8.30pm that same evening 3 shots were fired into a window of the East Wind Bookshop, Brisbane. The shop being known for its links and support of the Communist movement. At 9pm the same male again telephoned the news desk of the Courier-Mail newspaper and said:

"We are members of an extreme right-wing group. I spoke to you earlier in the night after we blew up the Communists Party Headquarters. Now we have shot up the East Winds Bookshop. We are doing this to stop the red rats marching on Friday. We tried not to hurt anyone."

The twin attacks were significant, evoking an immediate response from the Queensland authorities. A prime suspect was identified but he had fled interstate immediately following the attacks. The suspect was arrested and extradited back to Queensland where he was committed for trial.

The suspect had previously been a member of the Brisbane branch of the National Socialist Party of Australia (NSPA) but had been dispelled from the branch for conduct unbecoming of a national socialist (neo-Nazi). The suspect then established his own neo-fascist group. It was alleged that the bombing was conducted under the guise of this new group.

During the trial a legal technicality was discovered which resulted in the suspect being acquitted of all offences relating to the twin attacks.

Figure 5.3: Characteristics (XLW) Toolbox

Categories	Characteristics
Motivation	XLW are driven by support of their belief. They tend to promote the use of violence to achieve a 'noble cause'. The reliance on their noble cause (belief) enables them to promote their illegal actions from the perspective of acting on behalf of the greater good for minorities, humanity or the planet. However, this sentiment of the public good is generally self-focused and may be at the expense of other sections of the community. They are also influenced by conspiracy theories and they are intertwined with their opposing ideology XRW.

Leadership / Structure	These are decentralised autonomous groups. In general, they promote non conformity and disorder. Members' allegiance is primarily to the belief; however, leaders of these groups are usually charismatic. The structure of these groups tends to be stable and able to survive changes in their leadership. Their membership may consist of individuals considered on the fringe of society's acceptable norms.
Other General Characteristics	XLW has evolved from being motivated from a political perspective such as FARC, RAF and Action Directe that were prevalent in Rapoports' 'new left' during the 1960s–70s. These groups have now evolved to where they are now predominately motivated by contemporary social agendas.[18] Members of these groups are typically self-orientated, who apply a victim narrative to their belief and members. These groups are often goal–focused, with little empathy for other beliefs. XLW generally operate in groups subject to cognitive opening radicalisation.

---

[18] Rapoport, D.

An example of this form of motivation is set out below in the case study — Wobblies murder of Constable Duncan (XLW).

Case Study 18 – Wobblies Murder of Constable Duncan (XLW)

Background:

The Industrial Workers of the World (IWW) or 'Wobblies' as they were informally known, was an international labour movement that formed in the USA around 1905. Their ideology was a mix of socialism, anarchism and Marxism with the goal of ensuring industrial rights for workers through the use of violence and criminality. They were described as a revolutionary industrial union movement whose ideology evolved into becoming anti-establishment and anti-government. The Wobbies splintered and reformed spreading across America taking hold in numerous trades, industries and labour movements.

Details:

By 1910, the Chicago branch ideology of the movement had infiltrated Australia, establishing its head office in Sydney and spreading its tentacles across the entire country. In Australia the movement espoused industrial unrest, sabotage, arson and violence.

On 23 September 1916, in the middle of this evolving revolutionary unionist movement, a young NSW Police officer, Constable George Duncan was transferred from Grenfell to the one-man police station in the small central NSW rural town of Tottenham.

On 25 September 1916, Constable Duncan arrested and charged a local member of the Wobblies with indecent language. The following night, in support of their anti-establishment IWW beliefs, 3 members of the Tottenham Wobblies hatched a plan to murder Constable Duncan in retaliation for the arrest of their colleague.

At 9pm the same night while Constable Duncan sat typing at his desk, the three members of the Wobblies crept up to the small window of the Police Station, just 6 feet behind from where Constable Duncan was sitting. As Constable Duncan stopped typing and began to turn his head around, he was shot in the back twice with a third shot missing its mark. The 3 offenders immediately ran away leaving Constable Duncan to die a short time later on the floor of the police Station.

In October 1916, the three offenders were arrested and charged with murder. During their trial the Crown Prosecutor stated:

"...that the reason for this awful murder was the pernicious literature of the International Workers of the World. Both of the accused were members of this organisation. Both of them were young fellows whose minds might be inflamed and poisoned by the pernicious literature which they might read.... I think it will be abundantly clear that these men obtained the literature of the I.W.W..."

Their trial lasted one day, two of the offenders were convicted and sentenced to death the remaining suspect was acquitted. Constable First Class Duncan[19] was the first Australia Police officer to be killed on duty by an act of terrorism.

In December 1916 in the wake of the murder of Constable First Class Duncan and the unprecedented threat that the Wobblies posed to the community, the Australian Prime Minister, Billy Hughes being a member of the Australian Labor Party passed legislation that outlawed the Wobblies, identifying them as an unlawful association.

Figure 5.4: Characteristics (XIM) Toolbox

Categories	Characteristics
Motivation	XIM is frequently driven by an obsessive belief. It may sometimes be referred to as 'special interest terrorism', which covers a wide range of ever-evolving issues. While there may be several issues, generally, there will be a predominant belief that has precedence, which is not perceived as religious, political, left or right-wing. This form of belief is further aggravated by their perceived conspiracies. Examples may include pro/anti-abortionists, Incels, sovereign citizens, anti-vaxxers, cookers, etc.

---

[19] Constable Duncan was posthumously promoted to the rank of Constable First Class.

Leadership / Structure	These are decentralised autonomous groups. They may subscribe to a global ideology and network or may operate as lone actors. They follow a similar structure to that of the XLW in being organic, promoting non-conformity and disorder.
Other General Characteristics	Members of these groups are typically self-oriented, who apply a victim narrative to their belief and its members. These groups are often goal-focused with little empathy for other beliefs. Members may be susceptible to being obsessive in relation to their belief. XIM can be subject to fixated, mental health, and cognitive opening radicalisation.

An example of this form of motivation is set out below in the case study —abortion clinic attack (XIM).

Case Study 19 – Abortion Clinic Attack (XIM)[20]

Background:

Early in 2000, Peter James Knight, a 47-year-old fixated individual who resided in a make shift humpy in rural NSW, became obsessed with the 'right to life' movement. Knight commenced espousing his beliefs and conducting lone protests and demonstrations. A favourite site for these protests was outside the then popular Sydney radio station 2UE.

Details:

Early 2001 Knight attended the right to life offices in Melbourne where he made numerous requests, all of which were rejected by the movement. Knight's activities escalated, attending protests outside Melbourne abortion clinics. At some stage during these protests Knight developed a plan to conduct a massacre within an abortion clinic as a means to gain support for his crusade.

---

[20] R-V-Knight VSC 498

Knight returned to NSW and began planning for his attack. In preparation he made torches to set the clinic on fire, mouth gags and door jams. He also stole a Winchester lever action rifle together with ammunition and 16 litres of kerosene. After his preparations were complete, he returned to Melbourne.

About 10.10am on 16 July 2001, Knight entered the Fertility Control Clinic, East Melbourne, armed with his rifle and a bag carrying his equipment. At this time there were 15 staff and 26 visitors in the clinic, it was Knight's intention to kill them all. On entry to the Clinic he shot and killed the unarmed security guard, Steven Rogers, he then aimed his gun at a pregnant female patient when a struggle ensued between Knight and innocent bystanders, Knight was overpowered and detained until the authorities arrived.

During his trial the Crown Prosecutor said to the jury, *"He was very passionate about abortion – very much opposed – his position went past opposition to obsession."*

On 19 November 2002, Knight was sentenced by Justice Teague to life imprisonment with a minimum non-parole period of 23 years. During sentencing Justice Teague said, *"You were a loner on a personal crusade when you went to the clinic. Your crusade was to effect social change." "You went to the clinic with a plan for a massacre."*

The actions of Knight were motivated by his extreme interpretation of his anti-abortion beliefs.

5.6 Emerging Trends in Ideologically Motivated Terrorism

An emerging trend in the motivation and justification for extreme ideologies of XRW, XLW, and XIM is the tactic of exploiting the 'my truth' mantra to justify their position. The definition of truth is complex and has been examined for thousands of years. In the context of this book, it is defined as 'a fact or belief that is accepted as true'. This simple definition means that truth is subjective. So in reality, there is no absolute truth, which is why it is being exploited by these groups to justify their beliefs and actions. There are numerous examples of the subjective nature of truth, for example, flat earthers and Jewish holocaust deniers.

Society has always been subject to disinformation and manipulation. Former US President Trump so elegantly described this phenomenon as 'fake news'. The emerging trend is that ideological extremists employ disinformation and/or the 'my truth' mantra as a means to promote their belief to a broader audience while using it as a basis for falsely justifying their use of violence.

5.6.1 The Rabbit Hole

Ideologically motivated terrorism is prone to conspiracy theories. These ideologies utilise basic psychological principles in the form of conspiracy theories as a means to rationalise and justify their beliefs. This rationalisation, regardless of how tenuous the alleged links may be, make their belief palatable to the mainstream. Examples of this include the 'alleged 2020 rigged US Presidential elections' that resulted in the US Capitol riots in 2021, the dangers of the COVID-19 vaccines, and the existence of the 'deep state'.

'Going down the rabbit hole' is a metaphor used to describe when a conspirationalist starts delving into a never-ending warren of conspiracies with a view to finding proof that their belief is true. This process can further entrench the individual in their ideology and may escalate their behaviour. Through this process, the individual may become irrational and pose an indirect threat to those who oppose their belief.

5.7 Summary

Belief is the fundamental component that distinguishes terrorism and extremism from other types of crime. These unique offences must be motivated by either religious, political or ideological beliefs; otherwise, they are not terrorism. While religious and political motivations are generally self-evident, ideologically oriented beliefs can be complex and challenging for counter-terrorism professionals to define and label.

Instead of identifying the potential infinite number of ideological beliefs motivating terrorism, this book simply classifies them into three broad categories: Right Wing

Extremism (XRW), Left Wing Extremism (XLW), and Issue Motivated Extremism (XIM). These beliefs form the foundation of the motivation that drives an individual or group to engage in acts of terrorism.

5.8   Key Points

- Belief is the fundamental component that distinguishes terrorism and extremism from other types of crime.
- The term *belief* includes any religious, political, or ideological convictions of an individual or group and includes all beliefs that may make an individual susceptible to radicalisation.
- The term *extremism* in a terrorism context refers to a belief system that passively supports the advancement of a political, religious, or ideological cause through threats or actions as defined as a terrorist act under that jurisdiction's legislation.
- XRW is defined as an extreme interpretation of either conservatism, authorism, nationalism, traditionalism, protectionism, or order.
- XLW is defined as an extreme interpretation of either progress, equality, rights, or social environmental and animal welfare.
- XIM defined as an extreme interpretation of a predominantly single belief that is not considered religious, political, right wing, or left wing.
- This chapter examined two psychological forces of motivation, intrinsic and extrinsic motivation.
- Extrinsic motivation exists when the forces that drive the behaviour are external to the individual, including external factors such as punishments or rewards that influence the individual's behaviour.
- Intrinsic motivation exists when the forces that drive the behaviour are internal to the individual.
- The majority of criminal behaviour is motivated by extrinsic motivation; however, the majority of terrorism is

motivated intrinsically. Intrinsic motivation is considered the more powerful form of motivation.

- Going down the rabbit hole is a metaphor used to describe when a conspirationalist starts delving into a never-ending warren of conspiracies with a view to finding proof that their belief is true.

6

Radicalisation

6.1 Introduction

Radicalisation describes the process by which a person's mindset is altered to the extent that they move beyond lawful acts of advocacy, protest, dissent, or industrial action to committing acts of terrorism in support of a belief considered 'extreme'. This is a unique human-based process that remains constant regardless of the individual's extreme belief/s (motivation).

For a person to be considered a terrorist, they must essentially satisfy two components. First, the presence of an extreme belief. Second, the individual is radicalised, that is, prepared to engage in criminal activity to further that extreme belief. Radicalisation and extreme beliefs are two separate components in the individual being a terrorist. Hence, all terrorists are considered 'radicalised extremists'.

The radicalisation phenomenon has been dissected and discussed by academia to exhaustion for the past 20 years. However, due to the continuing nature of the terrorism threat, the focus of these academic discussions needs to shift towards the practical needs of the counter-terrorism professionals so they have greater application in the operational environment. It is in this vein that this book has applied academic concepts as the foundation for constructing practical radicalisation models that enhance the operational capabilities of counter-terrorism professionals.

The development of these models has established that there is not one form or 'strand' of radicalisation, but rather multiple, each being separate and distinct from the other, with its own characteristics and behavioural indicators.

The impact of this premise from a counter-terrorism professional perspective is far-reaching. If each strand of radicalisation presents differently, that is, each strand has its own unique characteristics and indicators, this will impact the practitioner's ability to identify terrorism threats.

The majority of the current threat, risk identification, and assessment tools are primarily based on the premise of only one strand or type of radicalisation. They do not generally acknowledge the existence of multiple strands of radicalisation, nor do they identify the different sets of indicators that apply to different strands. This failure to identify these different strands and their indicators could lead to a potential failure to identify and prevent acts of terrorism. This is considered a 'gap' in current protocols.

6.2 Strands of Radicalisation

The application of 'grounded theory' in examining the relationship between radicalisation and behavioural indicator lists against the dataset of counter-terrorism investigations conducted in Australia from 2002 to 2020 identified different 'strands' of radicalisation. Each strand was categorised, based on its characteristics and indicators. This process was a cross between a formal academic approach and an operational assessment. The result was an operational application of academic concepts to formulate practical radicalisation models that may enhance the operational capabilities of counter-terrorism professionals.

The application of this methodology at present has identified five distinct strands of radicalisation. These strands fall into two broad groups: traditional and emerging. The identified strands of radicalisation include the following:

- Generational
- Home-grown (cognitive openings)
- Fixated
- Mental Health
- Extrinsic

Generational and home-grown (cognitive openings) radicalisation are considered to fall within the traditional strands of radicalisation. These two strands, while having similarities, are separate. These two traditional strands comprise the majority of the instances of radicalisation in Australia today and are interrelated. For example, if an individual or couple is subject to the cognitive opening strand of radicalisation, their children subsequently may be vulnerable to the strand of generational radicalisation.

The emerging strands, fixated, mental health and extrinsic radicalisation, are not as common and require further research to develop their behavioural indicator lists.

The behavioural indicator lists currently used in Australia are predominantly focused upon home-grown (cognitive opening radicalisation) radicalisation with limited influence from the generational. This means the other strands (fixated, mental health and extrinsic) may be overlooked or not recognised by counter-terrorism professionals.

6.2.1 Generational Radicalisation

This strand of radicalisation is based on the concept of *Social Learning Theory* by Albert Bandura. This theory states that behaviour can be acquired through direct experience or by observing others.[21] In this instance, the terrorist behaviour or intent (radicalisation) is learned from the individual's family members and peers. The observation that terrorists have family members being either supportive and/or actively involved in similar terrorist behaviour would not come as a surprise to experienced counter-terrorism professionals. The correlation between family connections and offending has been previously identified.

In this model, the individual is driven to become radicalised through the social network and family bonds. This may be facilitated through the shared family values and the family's moral position in relation to the extreme belief.

---

[21] Bandura.

Generational radicalisation refers to when the radicalisation process has been passed down from generation to generation, and from family member to family member. Radicalisation is indoctrinated into the individual via social learning theory by family members through their actions, morals, beliefs, conversations, pressures, and upbringing.[22]

The individual subject to this strand is a rational and legitimate actor. It is their normal position or status quo that they are prepared to directly or indirectly undertake action or threaten action defined as a terrorist act to support their belief. Furthermore, they are considered legitimate, in that, they legitimately support their extreme belief. An example of this form of radicalisation is set out below in the case study — generational radicalisation.

Case Study 20 – Generational Radicalisation

Background:

After the rise of the *Islamic State* (IS) in Syria, an individual fled Australia using false documents to travel to Syria to join IS. As a member of IS in Syria and northern Iraq, this individual committed numerous atrocities and acts of terrorism on behalf of IS. Eventually, he was killed in Syria.

Radicalisation Pathway:

Prior to leaving Australia, this individual had a long history of espousing an extreme belief. As a child, he regularly visited a close family member who at that time was in custody for terrorism offences. His closest friend was a convicted terrorist, who travelled to Syria with him and joined IS, and was also later killed in Syria. This individual also had other family members throughout the Middle East who were alleged to have been involved in various terrorist groups as well as a significant large portion of his peers adhered to an extreme ideology. All of these associates significantly impacted this individual's ideology and radicalisation.

The unique characteristics of generational radicalisation are set out below in Figure 6.1 in an easy-to-use Characteristics (Generational Radicalisation) Toolbox.

---

[22] ibid

Figure 6.1: Characteristics (Generational Radicalisation) Toolbox

Characteristics	Demonstrate
Rational and Legitimate Actors	<ul><li>Consistent</li><li>Long-term views of their extreme belief</li><li>In-depth knowledge of their extreme belief</li><li>History of association with like-minded individuals and groups</li><li>Sense of legitimacy</li><li>Possession of extremist material</li><li>Support from family and peers</li><li>Long-term commentary on their moral superiority</li></ul>

6.2.2 Home-Grown (Cognitive Opening) Radicalisation

This strand of radicalisation is a hybrid model. It is acknowledged that this is predominantly based upon the model developed by Quintan Wiktorowicz in his book *Radical Islam Rising: Muslim Extremism in the West.* This strand also includes aspects of the model developed by Mellis in *Amsterdam & Radicalisation: The Municipal Approach*, as well as adopting aspects from the field of 'Transformative Learning'.

Home-grown (cognitive opening) radicalisation typically encapsulates the circumstances when a member of society transitions from being a functioning member of society to becoming isolated and espousing extreme beliefs. This is a progressive model in which the individual advances from one stage of the process to the next along their journey to becoming radicalised or what is colloquially referred to as a 'terrorist'.

The model commences on the premise that the individual is a member of the community, who does not actively adhere to an extreme belief. The model is based upon the assumption that for reasons not yet identified, certain members of the community may be more susceptible to being radicalised than others. This increased susceptibility could be due to multiple factors such as culture, experiences, personality, and the level of an individual's resilience. The susceptibility component was introduced in the Amsterdam Model by Mellis as the 'breeding ground'. The individual's susceptibility is a complex issue; it is not proposed to address this in any further detail other than acknowledging that this model commences on the premise that the individual possesses a susceptibility trait to this strand of radicalisation.

The next step occurs when the susceptible individual experiences a significant or catastrophic event, crisis, or other factors that shake the foundations of the individual's previously held beliefs.[23] This experience may lead the individual to become open to alternative views or perspectives. Wiktorowicz identified this as a 'cognitive opening'.[24] This experience can be real or perceived by the individual; hence, it is a subjective process.

The individual progresses to the next step in which they now seek answers to their new internal dynamic.[25] At this point, they are referred to as 'seekers'. Operationally, this stage is regularly seen in individuals who transition from group to group and belief to belief before settling and adhering to one.

At this point, the individual is supplied or is exposed to various beliefs, activities, groups, ideologies, and lifestyles. For the purposes of this concept, these are referred to as material. This material may be moderate, which is acceptable within the parameters of the community, or extreme, considered unacceptable and no longer in line with the community's parameters based on the legal test being the 'reasonable person'.

If individuals are exposed to moderate material and they accept and adopt it, they are not a concern from a counter-terrorism professional's perspective.

---

[23] Wiktorowicz, Q.
[24] ibid
[25] Wiktorowicz, Q. and Mellis, C.

Conversely, if the individual is exposed to 'extreme material', which resonates with them, the individual may investigate and pursue this extreme material (belief) further as the possible answer they are seeking. At some point in the progression, the individual may or may not accept this extreme material. If the individual accepts it and commits to performing criminal acts to further that belief, they have become radicalised.

The latter stages of this model can occur simultaneously with the separate process of 'recruitment'. The recruitment process identified by Wiktorowicz bears similarities to this strand of radicalisation, but operationally, it is considered a separate process. The test for this position is that once an individual joins a group, the recruitment process ends; however, the radicalisation process continues indefinitely. An example of this form of radicalisation is set out below in the case study — cognitive opening radicalisation.

Case Study 21 – Cognitive Opening Radicalisation

Background:

A highly successful and intelligent professional from Pakistan immigrated to Australia to further his career. Unfortunately, at that time, his qualifications were not recognised by the Australian governing body for his profession. To practice in Australia, he was required to undertake further study. The individual successfully completed these additional studies but was still unable to find any work.

Radicalisation Pathway:

Financial difficulties caused by his inability to find work forced him to return to Pakistan. The venture was perceived by the individual as a failure; in his eyes, he had lost the respect of his family and friends. This event had a significant impact on him.

After returning to Pakistan, he returned to his religion and started attending various mosques. At some point, he attended a mosque controlled by the proscribed terrorist group Lashkar –e- Tayba (LeT). LeT espoused an extreme interpretation of Islam, which in part was anti-western. This interpretation resonated with the individual. Subsequently, he was recruited and became a member of this terrorist organisation. He later returned to Australia where he and others were convicted for planning to commit a terrorist act on behalf of LeT.

The unique characteristics of cognitive opening radicalisation are set out below in Figure 6.2 in an easy-to-use Characteristics (Cognitive Opening Radicalisation) Toolbox.

Figure 6.2: Characteristics (Cognitive Opening Radicalisation) Toolbox

Characteristics	Demonstrate
Rational and Legitimate Actors	• Change in behaviour • Presence of a 'corruptor' (either in the real world or online) • Strict adherence to new extremist belief • Withdrawal from existing social networks • Isolation with new associates • Possession of extremist material • Lack of in-depth knowledge of their belief • Black and white view • Vocal on new belief • Limited tolerance for those who do not adhere to the same belief • Attempt to coerce others to adhere to their belief

This Radicalisation Model process is set out below in Diagram 6:1 Home-Grown (Cognitive Opening) Radicalisation Model.

Diagram 6.1:

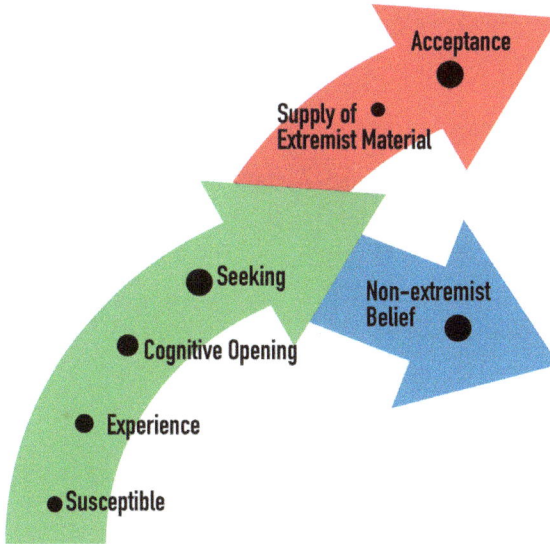

HOME GROWN (COGNITIVE OPENING) RADICALISATION

Illustrated below in Diagram 6.2 is the 'Integration Model', which incorporates the Counter-Terrorism Parameters with 'Home Grown (Cognitive Opening) Radicalisation Model'. This diagram demonstrates the progression of the cognitive opening radicalisation process overlaid against the operational parameters of counter-terrorism.

Diagram 6.2:

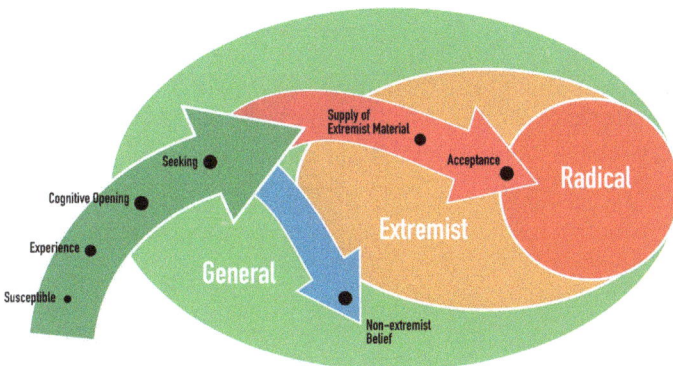

INTEGRATION MODEL

6.2.3 Fixated Radicalisation

This strand is based upon the concept of 'Fixated Persons'. This refers to individuals who present as fixated, who suffer from mental health or personality disorders contributing to their fixations. It is the fixation that potentially drives the individual's motivation to commit terrorist acts.

This book has developed a definition for a fixated person for the purposes of establishing context for the discussion, which has been derived from several sources. To be consistent with the main principle that terrorism is a criminal activity, this definition incorporates the elements of threat and public safety as a component for involvement by counter-terrorism professionals.

Fixated Person

A fixated person is defined as follows:

'A fixated person is one who suffers from a mental health or personality disorder that contributes to their obsessive pre-occupation of an organisation, individual, group, or belief to such an irrational degree that it constitutes a threat to the safety of an individual or section of the community.'

The rise in the public profile and attention of terrorists aligned with groups such as the Islamic State has seen the occurrence of infamy and recognition associated with those individuals. This infamy is attributed to the individual regardless of whether their acts were done with or without the legitimate authority of the terrorist group or their belief.

This infamy can be a motivator for those individuals identified as fixated. The result is that fixated persons, who have had no previous history of being associated with the terrorist belief or group, may now undertake acts of violence in the name of the terrorist belief or group. It is the position of this book that this is done as a means to attract recognition or the attention the fixated individual desires.

Fixated persons may act violently (acts of terrorism) in the name of that belief or group, but as they do not actually believe in it, they are for all intents and purposes 'fraudulent actors'. The result is that the indicators for their radicalisation process differ dramatically from the previously identified traditional forms of radicalisation.

One of the significant characteristics of this strand of radicalisation is the presence of either a mental health or personality disorder. An example of this strand of radicalisation was demonstrated by Man Monis during the Lindt Cafe siege in 2014 as set out in the case study—fixated radicalisation.

Case Study 22 – Fixated Radicalisation (Monis)

Background:

On 15 December 2014, Man Monis, armed with a sawn-off shotgun and a backpack that was reasonably suspected of containing explosives, took several hostages at the Lindt café, Sydney. During the siege, Monis displayed a black flag depicting a form of Arabic writing, which is commonly referred to as the 'Shahada'. The black flag in this format was associated with the terrorist group Al Qaeda (AQ) and Osama Bin Laden. However, Monis stated that he was acting on behalf of the Islamic State (IS) and wanted authorities to provide him with an IS flag. On 16 December 2014, the siege was resolved; however, it resulted in the deaths of two innocent hostages and Monis.

Radicalisation Pathway:

At the coronial inquest, the following issues were ascertained in relation to his radicalisation: Monis had a history of mental illness. He displayed signs of fixation, there was limited evidence of traditional indicators of radicalisation, no identified links to IS, the speed of his radicalisation, lack of evidence of his alignment to the ideology of IS, and his limited possession of extremist material. Independent to these issues the NSW State Coroner found Monis to be fixated.

The unique characteristics of fixated radicalisation are set out below in Figure 6.3 is an easy-to-use Characteristics (Fixated Radicalisation) Toolbox.

Figure 6.3: Characteristics (Fixated Radicalisation) Toolbox

Characteristics	Demonstrate
Irrational and Fraudulent Actors	<ul><li>Suffering from mental health / personality disorder</li><li>Speed of radicalisation</li><li>Inappropriate, harassing, or threatening communications</li><li>Stalking</li><li>Irrational (fixated) motivation</li><li>Signs of delusion</li><li>Grievance or perceived injustice</li><li>Display of anger, violence, or aggression</li><li>Isolation</li><li>Lack of or limited possession of extremist material</li><li>Lack of association with extreme belief and material</li><li>Escalating behaviour</li><li>Display obsession</li><li>End of day's commentary</li><li>Chaotic individual.</li></ul>

6.2.4 Mental Health Radicalisation

This strand of radicalisation is based on the various aspects of mental health and their impact on motivating or causing the individual to act. It includes individuals who commit terrorist acts as defined in each jurisdiction's legislation. In relation to this strand of radicalisation, it is the individual's mental illness that drives or motivates them to commit acts, as opposed to any legitimate support for the belief they allege to be acting on. This strand does not include fixated persons.

Traditionally, these individuals are not considered terrorists. However, if a person suffering from a mental illness conducts an act technically defined as an act of terrorism, regardless of whether they legitimately support the belief or not, in the eyes of the community or by applying the 'pub test', it will be considered an act of terrorism.

This strand of radicalisation presents differently from traditional strands of radicalisation. It can be argued that it follows a process similar to fixated radicalisation, with a potentially short timeframe for radicalisation and a lack of legitimate support for the belief. Consequently, there may be little evidence of these individuals previously being associated with the extreme belief or terrorist group. These individuals are usually classed as committing a terrorist act but are not considered terrorists in that they do not legitimately support the belief. An example of this form of radicalisation is set out below in the case study — mental health radicalisation.

Case Study 23 – Mental Health Radicalisation

Background:

In 2016, a young person posted on social media their intention to conduct a terrorist act by randomly killing people in the Sydney CBD. Members of the Joint Counter-Terrorism Team (JCTT) and local police intervened and interviewed the young person. During the interview, the young person admitted their intention to conduct a terrorist attack. The purpose of this act was to raise public attention for mental health and youth suicide.

Radicalisation Pathway:

The youth was initially charged with terrorism offences. However, further inquiries revealed that the individual was suffering from mental health issues. These mental health issues were identified as the cause of their intended actions. As proceedings continued, it was established that due to mental health issues, they were unable to meet the threshold for being able to commit a criminal offence. The terrorism charges were withdrawn, and the young person was treated under appropriate mental health legislation.

The unique characteristics of mental health radicalisation are set out below in Figure 6.4 is an easy-to-use Characteristics (Mental Health Radicalisation) Toolbox.

Figure 6.4: Characteristics (Mental Health Radicalisation) Toolbox

Characteristics	Demonstrate
Irrational and Fraudulent Actors	• Suffering from mental health • Speed of radicalisation • Lack of association with extreme belief /material • Display of violence • Escalating behaviour • Copycat behaviour • Signs of delusion • Chaotic individual

6.2.5 Extrinsic Radicalisation

This strand of radicalisation is based on the concept of 'Extrinsic Motivation'. This refers to behaviours that are driven by pressures, obligations and constraints from external sources. This is behaviour driven by either rewards or punishment. This may be referred to as either the carrot (reward) or stick (punishment) approach. This strand of radicalisation is uncommon in Australia. However, it is regularly seen in other parts of the world, especially those considered to have a low socio-economic lifestyle.

This form of radicalisation presents differently from the traditional forms of radicalisation. Individuals subject to this form of radicalisation are considered rational actors but may be either legitimate or fraudulent actors. Generally, they make calculated decisions based on their own needs versus potential risks. An example of this form of radicalisation is set out below in the case study — extrinsic radicalisation.

Case Study 24 – Extrinsic Radicalisation (Islamic State)

Background:

Terrorist groups such as Islamic State (IS) at certain times have engaged in operations and taken control over particular regions. In these regions when controlled by groups such as IS, they have acted as the pseudo-government. On occasion, IS has paid its fighters a salary of between $US400–$US1,200 a month, plus additional monthly payments of $US50 per wife and $US20 per child.

Radicalisation Pathway

In several countries, these amounts are significantly higher than the average national salary. Information from authorities in these countries reveals that they had a number of their nationals travelled to Syria and engage in terrorist acts on behalf of IS, primarily for the financial (extrinsic) rewards.

The unique characteristics of extrinsic radicalisation are set out below in Figure 6.5 is an easy-to-use Characteristics (Extrinsic Radicalisation) Toolbox.

Figure 6.5: Characteristics (Extrinsic Radicalisation) Toolbox

Characteristics	Demonstrate
Rational - Legitimate / Fraudulent Actors	• Rational calculating behaviour • Presence of an external motivator • Maintenance of known established social networks • Consistent behaviour • Suspicious of authorities • Calculated decisions influenced by external factors

6.3 Methods of Radicalisation

The basic methods used to radicalise individuals (regardless of the radicalisation strand) will be referred to as the methods of radicalisation. These methods should be considered as forms of evidence that need to be identified and captured by the relevant counter-terrorism collection capability. Some of these methods may include the following:

- Existence of a corruptor
- Extremist material
- Association
- Isolation
- Speeches, comments or postings by prominent individuals
- Cyber or social media

6.4 Behavioural Indicators

Due to the dynamic nature of terrorism, there is currently no single terrorist personality or single effective process for profiling terrorists. However, there are several indicators or acts committed by radicalised extremists that share commonality in relation to suspected terrorist activity. These indicators or acts include trends seen in the radicalisation processes.

The identification of these indicators by collection capabilities may provide a basis for determining if a person is radicalised or is susceptible to radicalisation. Counter-terrorism professionals may use these indicators as a tool to anticipate the person of interest's (POI's) state of mind and/or intention. The presence of a number of these indicators is not necessarily proof that the individual is radicalised; rather, it provides an indication that requires further assessment by an experienced counter-terrorism professional as to their significance. A list of unique behavioural indicators for each strand of radicalisation is documented below in the individual behavioural indicator toolboxes.

Figure 6.6: Indicators (Generational Radicalisation) Toolbox

Strand	Potential Indicators
Generational (Rational Actor)	• Behaviour and appearance consistent with an extreme belief (consistency) • In-depth knowledge of the extreme belief • Absolutist position • Vocalisation of belief • Attempts at coercion of those around them to follow the extreme belief • Disputation with those who do not support their belief • Disputation with those following a less 'extreme' version of the same ideology / belief • History of association with individuals adhering to the extreme belief • Support from family and peers • Possession of extremist material • History of exchanging extremist material • Position of moral superiority over, or hatred towards other groups • History of non-acceptance of the legitimacy of authority • History of promoting violence to advance extreme belief • History of committing minor offences • Physical preparation and/or training for an act of violence • Preparations for an act of terrorism

Figure 6.7: Indicators (Cognitive opening Radicalisation) Toolbox

Strand	Potential Indictors
Cognitive Opening (Rational actor)	• Experience of a significant events preceding the adherence to the new extreme belief • Change in behaviour • Appearance in line with adherence to extreme group or belief • Vocal about adherence to a new belief • Lack of in-depth knowledge of the belief • Existence of a corruptor (maybe a recruiter) • Attempts at coercion of those around them to follow an extreme ideology • Disputation with close personal relationships based on extreme behaviour or ideas • Disputation with those following a less 'extreme' version of the same ideology or belief • Withdrawal from existing social activities or friends • Close connection to individuals already radicalised • Commitment of loyalty, pledge, or initiation to extreme belief • Isolation (this may be part of a group isolating) • Possession of extremist material • Exchange extremist material with others • Commentary of moral superiority over, or hatred towards other groups

- No longer accepting of the legitimacy of authorities
- Promotion of violence to advance extreme belief
- Commission of minor offences
- Engagement in graffiti or signage – extreme messages
- Suspicion of attention from the authorities
- Confrontational or threatening behaviour
- Preparations for an act of terrorism

Figure 6.8: Indicators (Fixated Radicalisation) Toolbox

Strand	Potential Indicators
Fixated (Irrational actor)	• Suffering from a mental illness or condition that directly contributes to their behaviour (may include cognitive distortion and personality distortion) • Fraudulent actor in relation to the belief • Lack of in-depth knowledge of belief • Inappropriate, harassing, or threatening communications • Stalking (physical, online, or by proxy) • Irrationality (in relation to the motivation for fixation) • Fixation or obsession • Signs of delusion • Existence of a grievance or perceived injustice • Display of anger or aggression • Display of violence (including domestic violence) • Isolation • Subject to escalating behaviour

- End of days' commentary
- Chaotic individual
- Attacks against symbolic targets
- Violence against those that hinder their activities
- Probable substance abuse
- Preparations for a terrorist act

Figure 6.9: Indicators (Mental Health Radicalisation) Toolbox

Strand	Potential Indicators
Mental Health (Irrational actor)	- Suffering from a mental illness or condition which directly attributes to their behaviour - Irrationality (in relation to the motivation) - Signs of delusion - Display of anger or aggression - Fraudulent actor in relation to belief - Display of violence (including domestic violence) - Isolation - Subject to escalating behaviour - Chaotic behaviour - Lack of in-depth knowledge of the belief - Nil or limited history of support for belief - Lack of or limited possession of extreme material - Commentary of end of days - Probably subject to substance abuse - Preparations for a terrorist act

Figure 6.10: Indicators (Extrinsic Radicalisation) Toolbox

Strand	Potential Indicators
Extrinsic (Rational actor)	• Rational, calculating individual • Probable support for extreme belief • Consideration of the risks • Pragmatism • Maintenance of social networks or communications • Consistency • Increased suspicion of attention from the authorities • Recognition of the legitimacy of government and society • Preparation to commit criminal acts for a price • Commission of acts in preparation for a terrorist act • Preparations for a terrorist act

6.5 Summary

Radicalisation describes the process by which a person's mindset is altered to the extent that they move beyond lawful acts of advocacy, protest, dissent or industrial action to commit acts of terrorism in support of a belief considered 'extreme'. This is a unique human-based process that remains constant regardless of the individual's extreme belief/s (motivation). Radicalisation and extreme beliefs are two separate components in the individual being a terrorist. Hence, all terrorists are considered to be 'radicalised extremists'.

This book applies academic concepts as the foundation for constructing practical radicalisation models to enhance operational capabilities. The development of these models has established that there is not one form or 'strand' of radicalisation but rather multiple strands, each separate and distinct from the other, each with its own characteristics and behavioural indicators.

The impact of this premise from a counter-terrorism professional perspective is far-reaching. If each strand of radicalisation presents differently, that is, each strand has its own unique characteristics and indicators, this will impact the practitioner's ability to identify terrorism threats.

The majority of the current threat, risk identification and assessment tools are primarily based on the premise of only one strand or type of radicalisation. They do not generally acknowledge the existence of multiple strands of radicalisation, nor do they identify the different sets of indicators that apply to different strands. This failure to identify these different strands and their indicators could lead to a potential failure to identify and prevent acts of terrorism. This is considered a 'gap' in current protocols.

This book has identified five distinct strands of radicalisation. These strands fall into two broad groups: traditional and emerging. Traditional includes generational and home-grown radicalisation. Emerging includes fixated, mental health and extrinsic radicalisation.

Due to the dynamic nature of terrorism, there is currently no one single terrorist personality or one single effective process for profiling terrorists. However, there are several indicators or acts committed by radicalised extremists that have a commonality in relation to suspected terrorist activity. These indicators or acts include trends seen in the radicalisation processes.

The identification of these indicators by collection capabilities may provide a basis for identifying if a person is radicalised or is susceptible to radicalisation. Counter-terrorism professionals may use these indicators as a tool to anticipate the person of interest's state of mind and/or intention.

To assist, this book has provided multiple easy-to-use toolboxes which identify the unique characteristics of each strand as well as identifying the unique list of behavioural indicators for each strand of radicalisation.

6.6   Key Points

- For a person to be considered a terrorist, they must essentially satisfy two components:
    o First, the presence of an extreme belief.
    o Second, the individual is radicalised, that is, prepared to engage in criminal activity to further that extreme belief.
- *Generational radicalisation* refers to when the radicalisation process has been passed down from generation to generation, and from family member to family member.
- *Home-grown radicalisation* refers to progression where the individual changes from being a functional member of society to becoming isolated and being prepared to act on their newly adopted extreme beliefs.
- *Fixated radicalisation* refers to individuals who present as fixated, who suffer from mental health or personality disorders contributing to their fixations. It is the fixation that drives the individual's motivation to commit terrorist acts.
- *Mental health radicalisation* refers to the various mental health illnesses (except fixation) that impact on motivating or causing the individual to act.
- *Extrinsic radicalisation* refers to behaviours that are driven due to pressures, obligations, and constraints from external sources (extrinsic motivators).

7

Recruitment

7.1 Introduction

Recruitment is a process carried out by all organisations, which is essential for their future success. Recruitment in a terrorism context refers to the overall process of searching for potential members, identifying them, and persuading them to either join a group and/or support an extreme ideology. The aim for counter-terrorism professionals is to identify these stages as they provide potential collection points for the counter-terrorism collection capabilities against the persons of interest (POIs) or terrorist group itself.

Much like radicalisation, the recruitment process will be unique to the individual and has no set time limit. There are several different theories and models on group dynamics and recruitment. This book adopts a number of the concepts from the *Social Movement Theory* of recruitment, which is based primarily upon the work of Snow, Benford, McAdam, Fernandez, Wiktorowicz, and others.

7.2 Recruitment vs Radicalisation

Recruitment to a terrorist group or extreme belief is a process separate from radicalisation. Both are similar and generally occur simultaneously with one another. To differentiate between the two, radicalisation is the process by which individuals come to accept the need for, and are prepared to participate in, violence or criminal activity to further their belief. It is an infinite process (enduring threat) that continues to ebb and flow with the individual.

Recruitment, on the other hand, is a process of searching, identifying, and persuading individuals to join a group or belief. It is a finite process that ceases once the individual joins the group.

It should be acknowledged that the recruitment process primarily applies to those strands of radicalisation that deal with rational and legitimate actors, such as generational, cognitive opening, and extrinsic radicalisation.

7.3 Stages of Terrorist Recruitment

7.3.1 Stage 1: Presence of a Recruiter

The recruitment process can be either formal or informal. The formal recruitment process for a legitimate organisation is generally conducted by the relevant Human Resources Department in a documented and/or structured manner. The informal process for a legitimate organisation may be conducted by a nominated member of the organisation, who has the delegated authority to recruit. This authority enables the recruiter to undertake recruitment in an ad-hoc manner. Either formally or informally, there is always an identified recruiter or an authorised representative of the organisation.

The recruitment for terrorist groups is no different, whether through formal or informal processes. A person is always responsible for the recruitment of the POI. The identification of the recruiter is significant as it may identify several important collection points. This process is set out below in the case study — presence of a recruiter (Pendennis).

Case Study 25 – Presence of a Recruiter (Pendennis)

Background:

In 2004, the Australian Islamic extremism landscape in Sydney and Melbourne saw the emergence of a self-appointed Sheikh, Nacer Benbrika (Benbrika), who espoused an extreme interpretation of Islam. Benbrika recruited followers to his cause, simultaneously establishing two separate terrorist cells, in Melbourne and Sydney. The purpose of these two cells was to conduct terrorist attacks.

Recruitment Pathway:

Benbrika was a charismatic individual who greatly influenced younger members who supported his ideology. This allowed him to exploit his influence

---

and recruit these young members who were at vulnerable stages in their lives. The result being that the members of both the Sydney and Melbourne cells were under the instruction and direction of Benbrika. The authorities eventually thwarted Benbrika's intended attacks which saw the cell members in Melbourne and Sydney arrested and incarcerated for extended periods of time.

7.3.2 Stage 2: Searching

In searching through the pool of candidates, numerous factors such as the belief, exposure, and associates of the potential recruit will have an influence on the terrorist groups recruitment. The larger the pool of potential candidates the greater the likelihood of success for that group. Wiktorowicz's model of recruitment for 'high-risk activism for radical Islamic groups'[26] identified that the process of searching was conducted through the social networks of members of the group. Wiktorowicz identified social ties as a primary avenue for recruitment. The stronger the social tie, the greater the potential for influencing and recruiting the individual.

Social networks are necessary for joining or being recruited to an organisation. There needs to be some amount of social contact or networking with a terrorist group, either in person or online. Wiktorowicz identified that 'no network = no recruitment'. This interaction is a significant collection point.

7.3.3 Stage 3: Identifying

Numerous factors determine the identification of suitable candidates such as the circumstances and needs of the group versus the skills and capability of the candidates. This stage is driven by the needs of the group; however, the group's capacity to identify suitable candidates may be limited by the group's belief.

Before a candidate is considered suitable for a terrorist group, they must possess a similar ideology and/or be sympathetic to its beliefs. Wiktorowicz identified this aspect as 'frame alignment'. Frame alignment occurs when the movement's ideology and belief

---

[26] Wiktorowicz, Q.

system resonate with that of the individual.[27] At this point, the candidate may be either eliminated from the recruitment process or identified as suitable. Once a suitable candidate is identified and vetted, the next step is to persuade that candidate to join.

7.3.4 Stage 4: Persuading

A challenge in recruiting for terrorist groups is that the individual must accept the potential consequences of joining an illegal group engaged in high-risk activity. During this stage the recruiter may attempt to induce or persuade the candidate to join. Wiktorowicz identified these inducements as 'incentives' whose purpose is to convinced the individual to join despite the potential consequences of their intended high-risk activity.

Incentives that attract recruits will be unique to the individual recruits. Incentives may include spiritual obligations, spiritual salvation of self or others or satisfy self-interests, moral obligations and noble causes.[28]

7.3.5 Stage 5: Joining

At the conclusion of the process, a suitable individual may be identified from the pool of candidates. To be suitable, they must possess frame alignment with the belief of the group, be persuaded to join, and subsequently be accepted as a member by the group. At this point, the recruitment process ceases. However, the radicalisation of the individual continues. The recruitment is demonstrated below in the case study — recruitment process.

Case Study 26 – Recruitment Process (JCTT Operation Peqin/Fellows)

Background:

On 2 October 2015, a 15-year-old shot and killed an unarmed civilian police employee, Curtis Cheng, outside NSW Police Headquarters, Parramatta. The attack was identified as an act of terrorism. The young person was shot and killed by Special Constables tasked with protecting Police Headquarters.

---

[27] Ibid
[28] Wiktorowicz, Q.

Network:

Four adult offenders were held responsible for this cowardly attack. They knew the young person through their various social networks which included:

- Most of the offenders had previously attended the same school.
- The young person's older brother was a known associate of the offenders.
- One of the offender's younger brothers was at school with the young person.
- All attended the same mosque.

Recruiter:

The authorities identified one of the offenders as being the principle recruiter and corruptor of the juvenile. This offender was seen speaking with the juvenile approximately 30 minutes before the attack.

Recruitment and Radicalisation Processes:

The young person was an individual susceptible to cognitive opening radicalisation. It is suspected that whilst at the mosque:

- He was 'identified' by the group through social networks as a possible candidate to undertake the attack.
- He was 'selected' due to his age, availability and susceptibility.
- It is suspected that the 'recruiter' and others engaged the young person, persuading him to join their group through frame alignment and religious obligation.
- Simultaneously with being 'recruited' into the group, he was being 'radicalised'.
- Once he agreed to join the group, he was accepted as a member and the recruitment process ceased.
- However, the 'radicalisation process' continued up until approximately 30 minutes before the terrorist attack upon NSW Police Headquarters.

7.4 Other Factors that may Influence Recruitment

Several other factors may influence the recruitment of an individual into a terrorist group. Gaining some understanding of how these factors work in the terrorism context is also important so that they can be exploited by the collection capabilities.

7.4.1 Environment

This includes their physical environment such as their community, detention centres, educational centres, meeting locations, personal environment, belief environment, and online environment.

7.4.2 Peer Groups

Peer group members can significantly impact the recruitment process. Through group dynamics, the peer group can influence the individual's framing and incentives. They can also facilitate interaction and networking with extremist and terrorist groups. These groups are also susceptible to 'group think', which may also impact the recruitment process, as well as being a consideration for counter-terrorism professionals and decision-makers.

7.5 Collection Points

Identifying the stages of the recruitment process and other factors that may influence recruitment identifies potential collection points that can be exploited by the collection capabilities. These collection points may assist in providing information (evidence) on:

- Networks
- Extreme beliefs
- Intent
- Documents or supporting information
- Identities of the group

7.6 Summary

Recruitment is a process conducted by all organisations, essential for their future success. Recruitment for terrorist organisations is a persuasion process that occurs through various stages. Like radicalisation, recruitment is a unique path for each individual. While it is acknowledged there are several different models for recruitment, this guide has adopted numerous concepts from the Social Movement Theory of recruitment.

Recruitment, although similar and at times overlapping with radicalisation, are both separate processes. Radicalisation is the process by which individuals come to accept the need for, and are prepared to participate in, violence or criminal activity to further their belief. It is an enduring process (enduring threat) that continues to ebb and flow within the individual.

On the other hand, recruitment is a process of searching, identifying, and persuading individuals to join a group or belief. It is a finite process that ceases once the individual joins the group. It should be acknowledged that the recruitment process primarily applies to those strands of radicalisation that deal with rational and legitimate actors, such as generational, cognitive opening, and extrinsic radicalisation.

7.7 Key Points

- Recruitment is a finite process, unique to the individual.
- Recruitment and radicalisation can occur simultaneously with each other.
- Recruitment in a terrorism context focuses on persuading potential members to join an activity that has high risk of consequences.
- Recruitment ends when the individual is accepted into the group.
- Stages of the recruitment process include:
  - Presence of a recruiter
  - Searching
  - Identifying
  - Persuading
  - Joining
- To be recruited there must be frame alignment with the belief of the group in conjunction with some degree of social network.
- Other factors that can influence recruitment such as, environment and social networks.
- The recruitment process provides numerous collection points that counter terrorism collection capabilities can exploit.

8

Threat and Risk vs Corporate and Public Safety

8.1 Introduction

Threat and *risk* are important and complex processes in the counter-terrorism management continuum. They are separate but complement each other in presenting an integrated picture of dangers, probabilities, and consequences to decision-makers.[29]

Threat and risk are predictive concepts and can be used for the allocation and prioritisation of resources. In an Australian context, this prioritisation is based on determining ratings or assigning values to either threat or risk. Whilst this seems a rational approach, the application of these processes can often be misused and/or misunderstood.

To assist counter-terrorism professionals and decision-makers in effectively navigating these processes, this book has adopted the following principles on threat and risk in relation to terrorism.

Terrorism Threat and Risk Principle 1

Risk is best applied to protecting the organisation, minimising the corporation's exposure to the dangers of terrorism.

RISK = CORPORATE SAFETY

---

[29] Tusikov, N.,Fahlman, R.

<u>Terrorism Threat and Risk Principle 2</u>

Threat is best applied to anticipating and protecting the community, minimising the public's exposure to the dangers of terrorism.

THREAT = PUBLIC SAFETY

To assist in understanding, these principles are demonstrated in the following scenario on the principles of threat and risk.

Scenario – Principles of Threat and Risk

Background:

An environmental activists group starts targeting a multi-national mining company. After a couple of months of protest action, the business practices of the mining company do not change. A small group of members from the original activists group believe that they need to escalate their protests, the rest reject this proposal.

The members wanting to escalate their protest activity form a new group that adheres to an extreme ideology. Their actions escalate to a point where members of this new group threaten to conduct terrorist attacks to destroy assets belonging to the mining company, as well as killing any employee of the company who they believe is engaged in any mining activity.

Safety of the Employees:

Applying the principles of threat, the components of likelihood (intent and capability) are better suited to managing the safety of the employees (public).

Safety of the Mining Company:

Applying the principles of risk, the components of likelihood in conjunction with the consequence are better suited to protecting the multiple corporate interests of the mining company from the dangers of a terrorist attack by the members of the environmental group.

To explain the application of these two principles in further detail, this book will examine the various applications of threat and risk to identify their limitations and suitability in managing public and corporate safety from terrorism.

8.2 Risk

Risk is a concept frequently used to manage the dangers associated with various phenomena. It comprises many different components. Standards Australia defines risk as the 'effect of uncertainty on objectives'.[30] From a counter-terrorism professional's perspective, risk can be considered the probability of a terrorist act occurring and its impact on the community and/or organisation. Risk may be expressed as follows:

RISK (Terrorist Act) = Consequence + Likelihood (Threat)

Risk management principles within the Australian jurisdiction are governed by Australian Standards (AS) and New Zealand Standards (NZS), which also include standards from the International Organisation for Standardisation (ISO) - specifically AS/NZS ISO 31000:2009. This standard has been adopted by Australian organisations engaged in counter-terrorism activities. The desired outcome of applying this risk process is to evaluate risk.

8.2.1 Risk Assessment (Rating)

Risk assessment combines previous assessments to provide a comprehensive portrait of the risk.[31] Standards Australia define risk assessment as '...the overall process of risk identification, risk analysis and risk evaluation.'[32] From a counter-terrorism professional's perspective, the purpose of a risk assessment is to determine a 'risk rating' for a potential terrorist event. Determining a risk rating enables decision-makers to identify and prioritise the appropriate resources to manage and/or mitigate that risk.

---

[30] AS/NZS ISO
[31] Leson, J.
[32] AS/NZS ISO

In this process, a risk rating is determined by plotting the two risk variables, consequence and likelihood, individually into a matrix. The point where these two values intersect on the matrix determines the risk rating. This rating assists the decision-making process related to that risk, meaning that risk rating matrices are intended as decision-support tools (see a later chapter on decisions). This process is depicted below in Diagram 8.1:

Diagram 8.1: Example of risk rating matrix

Consequence					
Likelihood	**Insignificant**	**Minor**	**Moderate**	**Major**	**Catastrophic**
Almost certain	Moderate	High	Extreme	Extreme	Extreme
Likely	Moderate	High	High	Extreme	Extreme
Possible	Low	Moderate	High	Extreme	Extreme
Unlikely	Low	Low	Moderate	High	Extreme
Rare	Low	Low	Moderate	High	High

The practical application of the risk assessment process is demonstrated above in Diagram 8.1. The calculated value for the variable consequence is 'moderate', and the calculated value for the variable likelihood is 'unlikely'. These two variables are plotted onto a matrix, providing a risk rating of 'moderate'. This rating is then used to support the decision of determining what resources will be required to manage or mitigate that risk.

8.3 Suitability of Risk for Managing Corporate Safety

The dangers of terrorism pose a significant corporate risk to organisations. The application of the equation of likelihood and consequence is well suited to the economic environment in minimising the dangers to the corporation. These dangers can adversely impact organisational reputation, market share, human resources, and financial and corporate liability resulting from a terrorist attack. An example of the appropriate application of risk to manage corporate safety is demonstrated below in the case study — corporate risk (terrorism) Australian Reinsurance Pool Corporation.

Case Study 27 – Corporate Risk (Terrorism)

The Australian Reinsurance Pool Corporation.

Background:

Prior to the terrorist attacks of 11 September 2001 (9/11), terrorism insurance was incorporated into the majority of standard insurance policies. However, In the wake of the catastrophic financial losses due to 9/11, insurers limited their liability in relation to terrorist events as there was no affordable reinsurance cover for terrorism risk.

Result:

This situation caused a financial risk to Australian corporations by leaving them financially vulnerable to the impacts of terrorism from an insurance perspective.

Solution:

To maintain a functioning economy that could mitigate terrorism risk and ensure corporate safety, the Australian Government passed the *Terrorism Insurance Act 2003, resulting* in the establishment of the Australian Reinsurance Pool Corporation (ARPC). The Australian Government guaranteed the insurance industry a liability of A$10 billion in the event of a declared terrorist event. This solution provided appropriate coverage to the insurance industry, which enabled them to offer policies to Australian corporations covering their potential financial risks arising out of terrorism.[33]

This book recommends that risk be applied to the management and mitigation of the dangers posed by terrorism to organisations (i.e., corporate safety).

8.4 Limitations of Risk for Managing Public Safety

The use of risk assessment tools such as the risk-rating matrix set out above in Diagram 8.1, whilst well suited to managing corporate safety is, however, poorly suited to assessing human-based threats such as terrorism. This is based upon the risk equation and its application to risk matrices, which will be explored below.

---

[33] The Australian Government

8.4.1 Risk Matrices

The effectiveness of the risk equation and subsequent risk ratings depend upon the joint distribution of the two variables, likelihood and consequence. It is essential that these two variables and their allocated values interact. However, in the terrorism context, the variable value for 'consequence' is static. That is, a terrorist attack has a predefined consequence (value) of catastrophic. Hence, consequence will always be treated as its highest value 'catastrophic' (one value).

This means the risk-rating process goes from an equation with two variables to an equation with one variable, likelihood. (NB: the components of likelihood constitute threat). If this one variable equation is applied to the risk-rating matrix, it impacts on the accuracy of the rating. This concept is demonstrated below in Diagram 8.2. Example of risk rating matrix – consequence rated at catastrophic.

Diagram 8.2: Example of risk-rating matrix – consequence rated at catastrophic

Consequence					
Likelihood	Insignificant	Minor	Moderate	Major	Catastrophic
Almost certain	Moderate	High	Extreme	Extreme	Extreme
Likely	Moderate	High	High	Extreme	Extreme
Possible	Low	Moderate	High	Extreme	Extreme
Unlikely	Low	Low	Moderate	High	Extreme
Rare	Low	Low	Moderate	High	High

Depending on the structure of the matrix, the above diagram shows that regardless of the value attributed to likelihood, the risk rating remains constant. Treating consequence at a constant level (value) restricts variation in the risk ratings, which diminishes its value as a decision-support tool.

8.4.2 Time-Consuming Complex Process

Counter-terrorism professionals operate in high-pressure, time-poor environments. Conducting risk assessments using matrices as shown above in diagrams 8.1 and 8.2, is a time-consuming process. Occasionally, they require multiple assessments of various components to determine the values of the variables 'likelihood' and 'consequence' before the rating can be calculated, assuming there are no information gaps.

This process also requires a separate risk assessment for each identified risk. Therefore, multiple matrices should be undertaken for each identified risk. Furthermore, every time new information is obtained, new assessments for each risk need to be conducted.

In this process, each risk is separate, and the treatment of each risk is specific to that risk, without necessarily relating to or impacting other risks. An emerging flaw in risk assessments for counter-terrorism operations is that the highest risk rating of an identified risk is deemed to be the overall risk rating for that operation, resulting in disproportionate treatment of other identified risks.

8.4.3 Lack of Consistency

Risk assessments are subjective and prone to variations. The assigned values in risk assessments (such as 'unlikely', 'possible', 'minor', 'moderate', etc.) can be described as vague fuzzy descriptors, determined by the assessor's subjective judgments. This subjective process can lead to 'noise',[34] a term Kahneman, Sibony, and Sunstein used to describe the infinite factors causing discrepancies in an individual's judgments on the same set of facts.

The subjective nature of the process can also be manipulated by the assessor. The counter-terrorism professional can manipulate the process to achieve the desired result, potentially overstating some aspects of the information while ignoring or understating

---

[34] Kahneman, Sibony, Sunstein.

others. An example of a risk assessment being manipulated is demonstrated in the following case study — risk assessment (lack of consistency).

Case Study 28 – Risk Assessment (lack of consistency)

Background:

An Australian law enforcement agency was preparing to conduct a major counter-terrorism operation. Part of the preparations included conducting risk assessments on the persons of interest (POIs) and locations where the POIs were expected to be located.

Assessments:

The risk assessments were undertaken by a number of intelligence analysts. Due to the size and significance of the operation, these assessments were overseen by the Senior Investigating Officer (SIO). Upon reviewing the risk assessments, which were based on the same information, the SIO noticed discrepancies in the ratings. When reviewed by another analyst, the results differed again. The SIO interviewed each of the analysts about the discrepancies in their respective risk ratings. He determined that the main issue stemmed from the individual analyst's perspective and framing of the information, which resulted in different risk ratings.

8.4.4 Bias

Bias, including individual, organisational, and societal bias, contributes to variations in these assessments. Bias is accepted as a component of 'noise' as previously identified. However, its influence alone can impact the individual's assessment, further exacerbating the potential for variations in the process. An example of organisational and individual bias impacting risk assessment is set out in the following case study — risk assessment (bias).

Case Study 29 – Risk Assessment (Bias)

Background:

Police received information from an informant, leading to the arrest of an individual for terrorism offences. Subsequent investigations necessitated a search warrant for the offender's residence to retrieve incriminating evidence. Jurisdictional police policy required a risk assessment and approval from the Local Police Commander prior to executing any search warrant.

Facts:

The risk assessment accounted for the following facts:

• The residence was secured by police.
• The offender was in custody.
• The alleged intended terrorist activity was offshore.
• The offender had no onshore capability.
• The only occupant on the premises was the police informant.
• Police investigations determined the informant was a law-abiding citizen, motivated by a legitimate desire to prevent the offender from committing a terrorist act.
• The informant was in direct communication with the police at the scene and had identified the locations of the incriminating evidence. (Whilst the premises were safe and secure police were not authorised to enter the premises without a warrant).

Bias:

Per their policy, police conducted a formal risk assessment for officer safety. The risk assessment rating was determined to be 'low'. However, the Local Police Commander rejected the 'low' risk rating, arguing it was a 'terrorist offence'. The policy for officer safety in the case of a search warrant for a terrorism offence predetermined that the risk rating must be 'high'.

A 'high' risk rating necessitates a mandatory response requiring specialist tactical police to enter and secure the premises using special weapons and tactics. The Local Police Commander, who had the authority to override this response, refused to do so, citing the nature of the 'terrorism offence' regardless of the facts. This form of bias is colloquially referred to in operational terms as being 'overcooked'.

8.4.5 Adverse Impact on the Decision-Making Process

Risk assessments are primarily designed to support the decision-making process, which itself is complex and subjective. This will be examined in further detail in Part B: Decision-Making Process. When subjective decision support tools such as risk assessments are used, they can increase the influence of bias and variations in 'noise', potentially leading to flawed judgements and poor decisions. The impact of such factors is illustrated in the following case study — flawed decisions (Ruby Princess).

Case Study 30 – Flawed Decisions (Ruby Princess)

Circumstances:

The Ruby Princess, a cruise ship operating out of Sydney Harbour, found itself in the midst of the global COVID-19 pandemic. It departed Sydney on 8 March 2020, and during its voyage, many passengers reported suffering from COVID-19 symptoms. Despite these reports, the NSW Department of Health conducted a risk assessment for the cruise, deeming the COVID-19 risk to be 'low'. As a result, on 19 March 2020, the Ruby Princess was allowed to dock and disembark its passengers without quarantine.

Results:

This decision, which was based on a flawed risk assessment, contributed to the deaths of at least 28 people and the infection of 662 individuals with COVID-19. On 15 April 2020, the NSW Government established the Special Commission of Inquiry into the Ruby Princess. The inquiry found that the risk rating system used by NSW Health, which classified the Ruby Princess as low risk — requiring no action — was inexplicable, unjustified, and a serious mistake. This reliance on a flawed support tool resulted in a poor decision.

8.5 Threat

The process of creating an integrated picture of threat and risk begins with identifying the threat. A threat can be defined as '...a person's resolve to inflict harm on another'. It can also refer to a hazard. In a terrorism context, the concept of threat extends to include serious harm to a person or severe damage to property, causing death, endangering a person's life, creating a serious risk to public health and safety, or seriously interfering with, disrupting, or destroying electronic information, telecommunications, or financial systems. A threat may be represented as follows:

THREAT (Terrorist Act) = Capability + Intent

8.5.1 Actual Threat

A terrorism threat may also be identified as either an 'actual' or a 'perceived' threat. An actual threat occurs when collection capabilities identify a POI or group making a threat (intent) that would constitute a terrorism offence and has the means to carry it out (capability). An example of an actual threat is illustrated below in the case study — actual threat (Operation Silves).

Case Study 31 – Actual Threat (JCTT Operation Silves)[35]

Background:

In 2017, two brothers in Sydney were recruited by Islamic State operatives in Syria and attempted to bomb a commercial airliner carrying approximately 400 passengers travelling from Sydney to the Middle East. The plot was foiled by a diligent baggage check officer for the airline who challenged the innocent courier when he attempted to check in his overweight luggage.

Intent: (Actual)

The Sydney-based brothers had been recruited by their older brother who was fighting with *Islamic State* (IS) in Syria. The brothers communicated with each other via a social media platform. Together, they formulated their plan to bomb the airliner using another brother as a courier, who was to unwittingly carry the bomb hidden in his luggage onto the plane (intent).

---

[35] Zammitt, A. (2020)

Capability:

In April 2017, members of IS sent explosives to be used in the operation hidden inside a copper coil within a wielding machine via an international courier company to the brothers in Sydney. The brothers received the explosives and instructions on constructing the bomb. The brothers concealed the bomb in a meat grinder which was purported to be a gift for a family member in Lebanon. The secreted bomb was packed into the luggage of the innocent courier. The two offenders drove their brother to the airport with the bomb where he unsuccessfully attempted to board the plane (capability). The bomb was subsequently retrieved by the offenders and disarmed with the intent for it to be used in another terrorist plot.

8.5.2 Perceived Threat

A perceived threat occurs when the collection capabilities identify circumstances, history, or actions of the POI/group that a reasonable person would assess as a threat that would constitute a terrorism offence. Generally, this perceived threat is based on 'capability'. An example of a perceived threat is illustrated below in the case study on perceived threat (Operation Pendennis-Eden).

Case Study 32 – Perceived Threat (Operation Pendennis-Eden)

Background:

In 2005, Australian authorities were investigating two terrorist cells operating simultaneously in Sydney and Melbourne, both under the leadership of Nacer Benbrika. The investigation into the Sydney cell was codenamed 'Pendennis-Eden'.

Intent: (Perceived)

The Melbourne cell had articulated several targets for their terrorist acts. In contrast, the Sydney cell had not identified or nominated a specific target. Members of the group upheld an extreme ideology (corrupted interpretation of Islam) that supported the use of violence to advance their beliefs. Collectively, they stored over 3.5 terabytes of extremist material on computers, frequently sharing such content among themselves. Members of the Sydney cell were connected to prior terrorist plots. Several were affiliated with overseas terrorist organisations, and some received training from these entities. In their dealings, they adopted criminal tradecraft, using coded messages and encrypted phones.

Capability:

In November 2005, authorities executed multiple search warrants, uncovering more than 20 firearms, around 40,000 rounds of ammunition, several machetes and knives, evidence of the purchase or attempted purchase of 850kg of chemicals for producing explosives, timing devices, detonation devices, ignition apparatus, evidence of attempted IED construction, tools necessary for making IEDs, and possession of military-grade rocket launchers, which were not found.

Although no evidence pointed to a specific target, subsequent court proceedings convicted all Sydney cell members based on their terrorist intentions.

- Operation Pendennis was Australia's largest terrorist operation which was successfully undertaken by the extraordinary joint efforts of Victorian Police, AFP, NSW Police, NSW Crime Commission, AIC, Cth DPP and the Crown Prosecutors.

8.6 Threat Suitable for Managing Public Safety

Both actual and perceived threats, and their subcomponents of 'capability' (resources + knowledge) and 'intent' (desire + expectation), are intrinsically human-based and apt for evaluating a terrorist threat. The threat application is particularly potent in pinpointing, mitigating, and managing terrorist threats against the public. It operates on a straightforward binary proposition: a threat either exists or it doesn't. Once identified, mitigation and management measures can be activated.

The binary application of a threat offers numerous advantages over traditional risk assessment processes. Firstly, it remains consistent, less affected by 'noise'. Secondly, it's harder to manipulate. Thirdly, it's better suited to high-pressure, time-sensitive situations. Finally, being objective, it further minimises variations in evaluations.

111

8.7 Implications of the Terrorism Threat / Risk Principles

Applying these principles holds considerable weight for counter-terrorism professionals in deciding the best method to address and diminish the hazards of terrorism.

8.7.1 Terrorism Threat and Risk Principle 1

<u>Terrorism Threat and Risk Principle 1</u>

Risk is most effective when safeguarding an organisation, limiting the corporation's vulnerability to terrorism's perils.

RISK = CORPORATE SAFETY

This principle suggests that if the primary duty of a counter-terrorism professional or decision-maker is to shield the organisation from terrorism's risks, then RISK is the optimal method.

8.7.2 Terrorism Threat and Risk Principle 2

<u>Terrorism Threat and Risk Principle 2</u>

Threat is ideally employed to anticipate and safeguard the community, reducing the public's exposure to the dangers of terrorism.

THREAT = PUBLIC SAFETY

Conversely, if the main responsibility of a counter-terrorism professional or a decision-maker is to foresee and protect specific individuals or the wider community from terrorism's threats, then THREAT is the most suitable process.

Hence, organisations aiming to ensure public safety should utilise threat, while those focusing on corporate protection should employ risk. It's recognised that in practice, organisations will conduct both distinct threat and risk evaluations. These are separate yet complementary processes, offering an integrated depiction of risks to both the enterprise and the public.

8.8 Public Safety

Authorities, whether in the public or private sectors responsible for managing public safety, have traditionally utilised risk as their primary process. However, with the implementation of the 'Terrorism Threat and Risk Principles', these agencies might need to shift their focus primarily from risk to threat concerning managing public safety. This change will influence processes that were previously risk-focused. Some examples of these adjustments are highlighted below.

8.9 Enduring Threat

Recent global trends have pinpointed that one of the major dangers of terrorism arises from a concept termed 'enduring threat'. In the context of the principles mentioned earlier, this was previously termed as enduring risk. An enduring threat pertains to a terrorist act committed by a POI who has already been assessed or was previously of interest to authorities in a terrorism context, but was deemed at that time not to be a terrorism threat. This is also recognised as a residual threat (previously called residual risk).

The 'enduring threat' concept was introduced earlier in this guide when describing terrorism as a boundless issue. Once an individual is identified as a potential terrorist threat, irrespective of their position in the management continuum, that threat persists and is deemed enduring or residual. Instead of resolving the act, the approach to that threat falls within the management continuum as presented in Diagram 1: The management continuum for the life cycle of a radicalised extremist.

8.10 Threat Ownership

Collection capabilities, both from private and public sectors, are active throughout the management continuum. Every organisation and collection capability possesses distinct roles and responsibilities at each stage.

The general principle for ascertaining which collection capability or organisation assumes the ownership of the threat at any given moment hinges on who is accountable for that threat. As the POI transitions through the stages of the management continuum, the ownership of the threat will migrate. This transition of the threat from one capability to another, or from one organisation to another, as the POI progresses through the stages of the management continuum, is termed 'threat shifting'. In the past, this was labelled 'risk shifting'.

It is vital that collection capabilities engaged in this continuum recognise when the primary threat ownership has transitioned from one capability or organisation to another, that is, pinpointing who holds the primary threat at any particular moment.

8.10.1 Threat Shifting

Threat shifting can arise due to deliberate or inadvertent actions by capabilities or organisations. Such actions might involve the sharing or withholding of pertinent information that influences threat ownership. Every capability and organisation ought to be cognisant of the potential ramifications of their actions concerning transferring the threat, whether to themselves or other entities, either intentionally or unintentionally. An illustration of threat shifting is detailed in the subsequent case study on this topic.

Case Study 33 – Threat Shifting

Background:

On a Tuesday morning, the collection capabilities of a private-sector intelligence organisation detected detailed information identifying a POI as a terrorist threat. At 4 pm the following Friday, this intelligence organisation briefed the jurisdictional police on the new information and identified threat. The jurisdictional police now hold the primary responsibility for public safety.

Threat Shifting:

By passing on this information to the police at 4 pm on Friday, the intelligence organisation has effectively shifted the ownership of the threat from themselves to the jurisdictional police.

8.11 Summary

The concepts of threat and risk complement each other, yet they are distinct processes that are often misunderstood. To assist in navigating the best application of these concepts, this book adopted the *Terrorism Threat and Risk Principles.* That is, *risk* is best applied to protecting the organisation, minimising the corporation's exposure to the dangers from terrorism. Whilst *threat* is best applied to anticipating and protecting the community, minimising the public's exposure to the dangers of terrorism.

These concepts are meant to support the decision-making process, not replace it. This suggests that risk ratings and matrices should be employed as tools that assist in making decisions rather than as the primary determinants. Over-reliance on these tools for decision-making can be both hazardous and potentially perceived as negligent.

Terrorism is an ongoing issue, managed via the management continuum. This model presents a unique perspective in terms of enduring threats. An enduring (or residual) threat is one where an individual has been identified as posing a potential terrorist threat, and irrespective of how this threat is managed, the threat persists.

The ownership of a threat is determined by who shoulders the most significant responsibility for it. This ownership will shift in correlation with the management continuum as it progresses through its various phases. When the threat migrates from one capability to another, or from one agency to another, it is termed *threat shifting*. This indicates that the ownership of that threat has transitioned to another entity.

8.12 Key Points

- Risk might be seen as the likelihood of a terrorist act transpiring and its projected impact on the community and/or organisation.
- Threat can be defined as "...a person's resolve to inflict harm on another."[36]
- An actual threat emerges when collection capabilities pinpoint a POI/group making a threat (intent) that would be classified as a terrorism offence and possesses the means to execute it (capability).
- A perceived threat emerges when collection capabilities discern circumstances, historical events, or actions of the POI/group that a reasonable individual would interpret as a threat that would classify as a terrorism offence.
- Risk is most effectively utilised for the protection of the organisation, reducing the corporation's vulnerability to threats from terrorism.
- Threat is best used to foresee and safeguard the community, diminishing the public's vulnerability to threats from terrorism.
- Ownership of a threat is dictated by the individual, capability, or agency that holds the responsibility for that threat.
- Threat shifting unfolds through the management continuum and can be initiated by deliberate or inadvertent actions by individuals, capabilities, or organisations.

---

[36] Prunckun, H.

PART B

THE DECISION-MAKING PROCESS

PART B : COUNTER TERRORISM PROCESS " DECISION MAKING PROCESS"

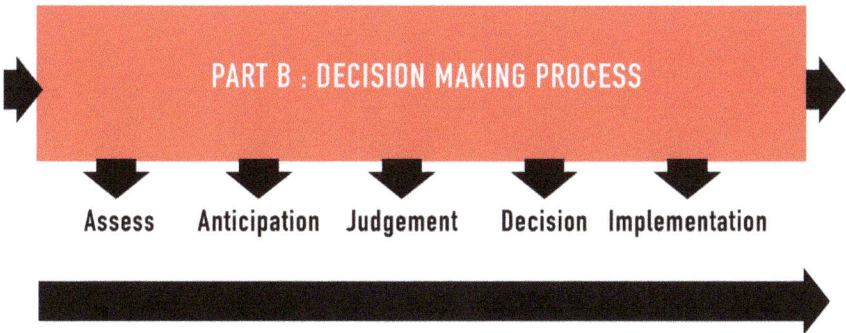

PART B : DECISION MAKING PROCESS

Assess   Anticipation   Judgement   Decision   Implementation

9

Assessment

9.1 Introduction

The next section of this guide examines 'Part B – The Decision-Making Process'. It is acknowledged that decisions are undertaken by both counter-terrorism professionals and decision-makers alike. However, this section targets the respective level of management in an organisation that bears the ownership of the consequences of their decisions.

The decision-making process is a complex progression, unique to each decision-maker. It commences with receiving and assessing the information, accurately judging the alternatives, and finally determining and implementing the optimum course of action. While several of these processes might occur simultaneously, they will be broken down into individual phases and examined for the purpose of this book.

Although the decision-making process has been tailored for the counter-terrorism environment, its principles are transferable and can be applied to other fields.

9.2 Assessment

The first step occurs when the decision-maker receives the information from the collection capabilities (Part A). This information can be relayed in various formats, including verbal comments, observations, reports, documents, footage, assessments, opinions, and options from the different capabilities. This might be communicated vertically, 'up through the chain of command', or horizontally from colleagues or other peer organisations.

The initial role of the decision-maker is to absorb the information to determine its significance, identifying potential threats and/or risks. While this seems foundational, it can be challenging to achieve due to competing priorities, workload, or other external factors leading to impaired judgements.

The ability to assess and comprehend information can also be impacted by its content. Under stress, decision-makers might filter out or rationalise what they don't expect or want to hear (i.e., problems). This tendency might impede the decision-maker's ability to recognise the information's significance or potential risk.

The manner in which the information is communicated also impacts on their ability to assess it. For example, verbal briefings may require a certain level of emotional intelligence by the decision-maker to pick up subtle non-verbal inferences. Conversely, a written report which is overly extensive or poorly structured can mean that the pertinent facts are lost in the text.

Efficient communication of the information from the collection capabilities (Part A) to the decision-makers in a timely and accurate fashion, lays the foundation for an effective decision-making process (Part B) whose purpose is the implementation of the optimum course of action through the management continuum.

10

Anticipation

10.1 Introduction

A terrorist attack is regarded by the community as a surprise. A surprise occurs when the outcome of an event is unknown. The success of a counter-terrorism professional and decision-maker relies on their ability to anticipate this surprise; that is, the ability to prevent the next 9/11, Bali (1) bombing or Hamas incursion attack. Thus, anticipation is a vital skill in the application of the management continuum. Anticipation in a counter-terrorism context is the process of looking forward to identifying and evaluating the future state of a potential threat.

Terrorism in Western societies is rare. Generally, Australia experiences a major counter-terrorism operation or attack every 6 to 8 months[37]. This infrequency results in small datasets on which to reply upon in order to anticipate these threats. The advantage of applying the elements of anticipation as set out here is that they are effective in applying to small datasets, such as those experienced in terrorism.

Anticipation in counter-terrorism is sometimes confused with other terms such as predicting and forecasting. Predicting in the criminal domain is based on making determinations by examining large datasets, like those found in high-volume crimes, including car theft, house break-ins, assaults, and theft. The term 'predicting' also suggests an absolute knowledge of future events which is inappropriate in this environment. Forecasting is a separate concept normally associated with determining future trends. This process is aligned to the strategic aspect of counter-terrorism, as opposed to the transactional nature of the management continuum. Anticipation

---

[37] Independent research by the author on Australian Terrorist activity 2002 – 2018.

in other contexts may also be referred to as predictive judgement, which will be addressed in the following chapter.

10.2 Elements of Anticipation

Anticipation is a cognitive skill used daily. Consider, for instance, making a cake with your kids. You ask one of them to return the jar of flour to the pantry. Observing them place the jar precariously on the shelf, you anticipate that it's likely to fall off, so you reposition the jar to ensure it is secure. Your anticipation and subsequent action prevented the jar from falling.

Given how frequently we employ our anticipatory skills, it's often mistakenly assumed that we are all proficient at it. Luckily, like all cognitive skills, it can be honed through practice, research, and training. The aim of addressing this principle in this book is to bolster this skill in decision-makers.

The elements that amplify anticipation include knowledge of the subject matter, behavioural indicators, history/trends, characteristics of the individual or group, escalation, change, time, and intuition.

10.3 Knowledge of the Principles of Counter-Terrorism

To effectively anticipate a threat, decision-makers must possess a competent knowledge of the subject. In this instance, principles of counter-terrorism as previously set out in this book. Without an appropriate understanding of these principles and the subsequent lessons learnt, the counter-terrorism professional and decision-maker may fail to recognise a situation, its reoccurrence or its potential significance when anticipating a future event.

10.4 Behavioural Indicators

There is no single terrorist personality or foolproof process for profiling terrorists. However, there are several indicators or actions committed by radicalised extremists that share similarities with suspected terrorist activity.

Identifying these indicators might offer a foundation for determining whether a person is radicalised or susceptible to radicalisation. Additionally, these indicators might reveal the intentions of the POI or group. Assessing these indicators by an experienced counter-terrorism professional is crucial for anticipating potential terrorist threats. An example of this element is illustrated in the following behavioural indicator scenario.

Scenario – Behavioural Indicators

Background:

The POI is an issue-motivated radicalised extremist (XMI), an obsessive anti-smoking extremist, vocalising a desire to eradicate tobacco from the community using violent means. A physical surveillance team provides the following observations:

08:00 – POI seen attending the city shopping centre.

08:20 – POI observed outside Shop 15, a cigarette specialty store.

08:25 – POI noticed making notes about shop attendants.

08:30 – POI observed noting the locations of security cameras.

08:50 – POI attempted to open the shopping centre's fire escape doors adjacent to the cigarette store.

09:20 – POI departed from the shopping centre, stopping at the external fire escape door he had previously tried to open.

09:25 – POI timed his walk from the fire escape to a car park two blocks away.

Comment by the surveillance team leader: The POI seemed to be conducting reconnaissance on the cigarette shop and its employees.

Anticipation:

The behavioural indicators suggest the POI might be planning a hostile act against the cigarette shop or its employees.

10.5 Characteristics of the POI/Group

10.5.1 Ability to Learn

Identifying the characteristics of the POI or group improves the ability to accurately anticipate future intentions. These characteristics can be multifaceted. For example, understanding a POI or group's ability to learn from experiences can shed light on their flexibility and adaptability. Recognising this trait will assist in anticipating their actions as situations change.

10.5.2 Personalities

Identifying personalities is fundamental for anticipation. It aids in discerning influences, group dynamics, motivations, individual roles, reactions to various situations, and tendencies towards action or violence.

An important aspect of personality assessment is determining whether they are rational or irrational actors. While a rational actor might be anticipated to react in a known manner to specific situations, an irrational actor's reactions are less predictable, potentially posing a greater threat.

10.5.3 Group Think

Group think, a psychological phenomenon identified by Irving Janis, describes conditions under which group members can make flawed decisions, suffer from reduced mental efficiency and poor moral judgement.[38]

When affected by group think, members fail to consider alternatives and/or tend to make irrational choices. Subsequently, the results of group think could have a significant effect on the intentions of the group, thereby impacting strategies employed by to counter their intentions.

Group think can occur in groups where there is directive leadership, high stress levels, external threats, isolation and there are self-esteem issues affecting members of the group.[39]These conditions may provoke a tendency for concurrence-seeking among members of the group, which may manifest itself as a series of group think symptoms.[40]

---

[38] Janis, L.
[39] Janis & Mann
[40] ibid

These symptoms may include the following: [41]

- A sense of invulnerability;
- Disregard for warnings;
- Perceived moral superiority, causing them to overlook the ethical or moral ramifications of their decisions;
- A negative attitude towards outsiders;
- Exerting peer pressure against dissenters;
- Self-censorship;
- An erroneous belief that their judgements are unanimous;
- Concealment of details to shield the group or leader from contradictory information.

Given the parallels with terrorist groups, members of such groups are prone to group think. Counter-terrorism professionals should be attuned to the conditions and symptoms promoting group think.

10.6 History and Trends

The Spanish philosopher Jorge Santayana y Boris (George Santayana) stated, "those who cannot remember the past are condemned to repeat it." [42]. Examining the history of terrorism assists the practitioner in better understanding how terrorists operate and function. It also provides an opportunity to learn from others and their previous mistakes in anticipating the future intentions of the POI/groups as they evolve.

10.6.1 Dates

History and anniversaries are significant to certain extremist beliefs. For example, the May 15 Arab Organisation was named after the date following the Independence Day of Israel (14 May). Black September was named after the month in which the PLO was driven out of Jordan. The 17 November Group was a Greek left-wing extremist group named after the final day of violent protests in Greece in 1973. 20 April marks Hitler's birthday. Such historical events and their anniversaries are salient to these beliefs and may incite specific behaviours.

---

[41] ibid
[42] Henfrey, N.

To assist, this book includes an annexed calendar toolbox. This calendar lists dates of significant terrorist events that might impact the Australian terrorism environment. Knowledge of these dates can help counter-terrorism professionals anticipate the influence these specific anniversaries might have on the behaviour of their POIs.

10.6.2 Trends

A trend within the terrorism environment denotes a prevailing tendency in methodology, capabilities, and/or targets. History has shown that the Australian terrorism environment often mirrors the international environment. Early identification of these trends is vital so that they can be recognised and mitigated before they manifest.

For example, in an Australian context crime trends will be unique to the jurisdiction. However emerging crime trends in Australia tend to initiate in the eastern states and migrate across the country. This is not an absolute but rather a general trend based on greater opportunities in the eastern states due to larger populations, more interaction with international markets and the flow of commerce.

10.7 Escalation

One of the most significant indicators of an increased terrorism threat is an escalation in activity. This can include communications, associations, surveillance, travel, internet activity, searches, purchases, religious worship, and more. Recognising escalation is vital in anticipating an increased terrorism threat.

10.8 Change = ▲

The identification of any change in this environment necessitates an immediate reassessment of the threat. Change in any aspect – including escalation or de-escalation, circumstance, context, dynamics, environment, intent, or capability – is significant in the anticipation of future actions or intentions of POI/s. The mathematical symbol for change is a triangle (upper case delta symbol), which will be used in an equation discussed later in this chapter.

10.9 Leakage

The term 'leakage' pertains to any actions or communications from POI/s that hint at their intentions. Typically, these intentions may be inadvertently revealed to others during interactions; that is, their intentions 'leak out', giving rise to the term 'leakage'.

10.10   Components of Threat

The concept of 'threat', defined as the intention to inflict harm, damage, or injury to another or others, is deemed a more pertinent approach concerning terrorism. Fundamentally, the components of threat, being 'capability' (resources + knowledge) and 'intent' (desire + expectation), offer a reasonably precise and reliable method in anticipating the terrorism hazard.

10.11   Time

The accuracy of assessing the likelihood of an event occurring (anticipation) increases over time. The closer the potential event, the more accurate the assessment is likely to be. This increase in accuracy is due to several factors such as more accurate and timely information, greater knowledge of capability, intent, and circumstance. This concept is shown below in Diagram 10.1.

Diagram 10.1

ACCURACY OF ASSESSMENT OF LIKELIHOOD OVER TIME

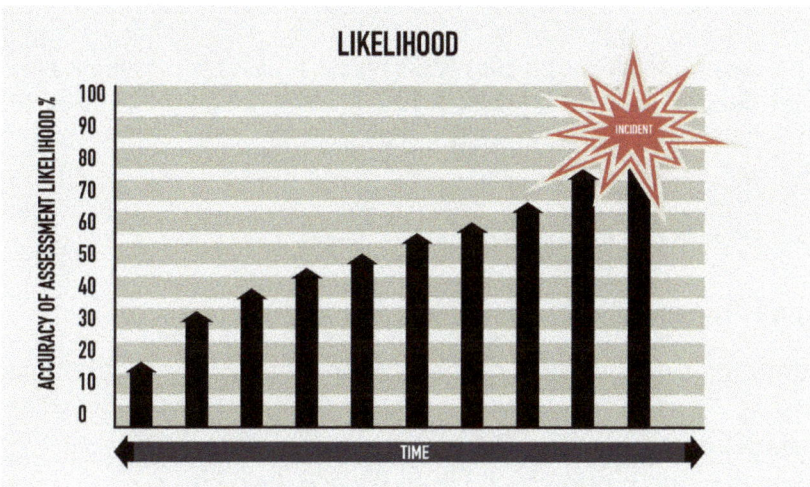

LIKELIHOOD

INCIDENT

ACCURACY OF ASSESSMENT LIKELIHOOD %

100
90
80
70
60
50
40
30
20
10
0

TIME

This concept is demonstrated in the scenario below on the accuracy of assessing likelihood over time.

Scenario – Accuracy of Assessing Likelihood over Time

Background:

On Monday morning, a teacher asks her students to anticipate the likelihood of rain at 9 am the following Monday (7 days later).

Assessment 1: (7 days out):

A diligent student considers several factors: the current season is summer, traditionally the wettest; the east coast of Australia is under a La Niña weather pattern, increasing the likelihood of rain; and it has been raining nearly daily for weeks. Consequently, the student anticipates a 95% likelihood of rain at 9 am in 7 days.

Assessment 2: (4 days out):

Consulting a weather forecast, the student finds a 70% chance of rain the next Monday. Given that it rained the past two days, the student adjusts their assessment to a 65% likelihood of rain at 9 am in 4 days.

Assessment 3: (2 days out):

The weather forecast now predicts a 45% chance of rain the following Monday afternoon. With no rain for the past two days, the student revises their assessment to a 35% likelihood of rain at 9 am in 2 days.

Assessment 4: (1 hour out):

At 8 am, just an hour before the predicted time, the teacher asks for a final assessment. The student observes clear skies and minimal wind. The weather forecast predicts a 40% chance of rain in the evening. Thus, the student assesses a 0% chance of rain in the next hour.

Result:

At 9 am, it is dry and sunny.

10.12 Intuition

Intuition is based on experiences, thoughts, observations and lessons learned. Sometimes, these lessons may have been assimilated subconsciously, without the individual realising. This phenomenon is referred to as *unknown knowns:* you're aware of something without realising that you are, hence, it remains unknown. Counter-terrorism practitioners and decision-makers sometimes refer to this as a 'gut feeling' or 'instinct'.

10.13 Ways to Improve Anticipation

Anticipation, as a cognitive skill, can be honed by integrating the elements of anticipation with consistent practice, training, and the employment of various models.

10.13.1 Scenario Training

Scenario training aims to foster 'what if' scenarios for professionals and decision-makers. This type of training, conducted via exercises, role-plays, and desktop simulations, allows participants to explore multiple alternatives and refine their anticipatory skills concerning evolving terrorism threats.

10.13.2 Use of Models

Anticipation, like many endeavours, can benefit from a range of models to bolster this skill. These models might be subjective or objective-based. They could offer a future probabilistic assessment or a fixed future time statement. Such models aim to forecast infrequent events, helping professionals and decision-makers best allocate limited resources and pinpoint actionable mitigation strategies. A pertinent example of model utilisation was Australia's response to the COVID-19 pandemic and the subsequent national vaccine rollout. Set out below are some examples of such anticipatory models.

Threat Model

The widely recognised anticipatory model is 'Threat', as delineated in the Australian and International Standards Risk Assessment Process. By their very nature, 'Threat' and its subcomponents, capability (resources + knowledge) and 'intent' (desire + expectation), are adept at assessing human-based threats and aiding in their anticipation.

Behavioural Indicator Models

These models, rooted in social science, focus on gauging observable events or activities. The data is then assessed for its correlation with preparations for a significant rare event, such as a terrorist attack. They might represent their findings in charts or similar visual aids, supporting the anticipation of the POI/s future intentions. An instance of this model type is the Terrorism Investigations Chart.[43]

Mathematical Models

These models utilise various mathematical techniques like algorithms, Bayesian equations, and game theory. Typically, these are effective for rational actors.

Insight Predictive Models

These models rely on experts visualising and probing a problem, using intuition to discern patterns. In a counter-terrorism context, these models depend on different experts interpreting the circumstances (data) in diverse ways, pinpointing patterns or probable intentions of the POI/group and guiding practitioners and decision-makers.

Conceptual Threat Anticipation Equation

This model was crafted for this book, intended to aid professionals and decision-makers in honing their anticipatory skills for the management continuum. The equation is depicted in Diagram 10.2.

Diagram 10.2 Conceptual Threat Anticipation Equation

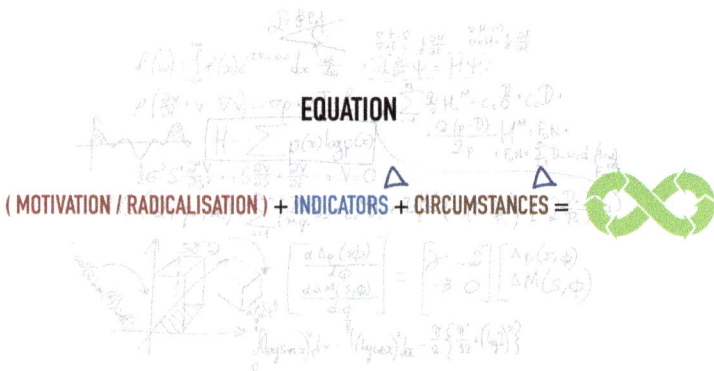

EQUATION

$$(MOTIVATION / RADICALISATION) + \overset{\Delta}{INDICATORS} + \overset{\Delta}{CIRCUMSTANCES} = \infty$$

---

[43] Gawel

Table 10.1 Key to Conceptual Threat Anticipation Equation

Motivation	Religious, Political or Ideological Extremism
Radicalisation	Generational, Cognitive Opening, Fixated, Mental Health, Extrinsic
Indicators	Intent & Capability
Circumstances	Subjective, Objective, Context, Circumstance
▲	Change
⬤⬤	Management Continuum: Life cycle of a radicalised extremist

10.13.3 Emerging Technologies

This refers to the application of evolving fields of study that can be applied to anticipation such as, computer science and mathematics. Examples of these fields include, artificial intelligence and machine learning. These emerging technologies offer enhancements in the ability to anticipate terrorist activity. However, it is acknowledged that these technologies have limitations due to the small datasets associated with the occurrence of terrorism within western liberal societies.

10.14 Summary

Terrorism in Western societies are rare events. Their occurrence is generally treated as a surprise. The ability to anticipate this surprise is a vital skill for counter-terrorism professionals and decision makers. It is the fundamental process that enables the identification and prevention of a terrorist attack. In the decision making process, anticipation provides the basis for making sound judgements which support good decisions that feed back into the implantation of that decision via the management continuum.

Anticipation is a cognitive skill which can be applied to every aspect of our lives. Like all cognitive skills, anticipation can be improved through practice, training and applying research. Elements which enhance anticipation in a terrorism context, include knowledge on the subject, behavioural indicators, history/ trends, characteristics of the individual or group, escalation, change, time, and intuition.

To effectively anticipate this surprise, it is proposed that decision-makers must possess a competent knowledge of the principles of counter-terrorism. Without appropriate exposure to these principles and subsequent lessons learnt the counter-terrorism professional and decision-maker may fail to understand or identify a circumstance and its potential significance, in anticipating a future event.

Terrorists don't fit a single mould, and profiling them isn't straightforward. This book suggests alternative strategies for anticipating their future intentions and actions.

10.15 Key Points

- Anticipation in counter-terrorism aims to foresee and evaluate future threats.
- It's pivotal in thwarting terrorism.
- Counter-terrorism professionals and decision-makers consider anticipation a vital skill.
- As a cognitive ability, anticipation can be refined through practice, training, research application, and models.
- Factors that bolster anticipation include knowledge of counter-terrorism principles, behavioural indicators, history, individual or group traits, escalation, change, time, and intuition.
- Ways to hone anticipation include scenario application, training, and model usage.

11

Judgements

11.1 Introduction

Judgements and decisions are complex cognitive processes. Both have been the subject of extensive academic research, particular concerning the different processes and their respective impacts on productivity and consequence. This book examines these processes from a practical perspective through the counter-terrorism management continuum.

The processes of judgement and decision-making are closely aligned but are separate. Both can be influenced by bias, noise, and other factors. This book proposes that both judgements and decisions are interrelated, intertwining multiple times throughout the decision-making process.

11.2 Judgement

Judgement as defined in this book, is a cognitive measurement of uncertainty, employing both objective and subjective methods. Its purpose is to form an opinion that underpins a subsequent decision. The goal is to arrive at accurate or sound judgements.

In a counter-terrorism context, the types of judgements include:

- accurate/sound judgements,
- inaccurate/unsound judgements,
- impaired judgements,
- professional judgements, and
- predictive judgements (anticipation).

11.2.1 Accurate/Sound Judgement

Accurate/sound judgement is the desired outcome of the process. Here, the decision-maker's cognitive assessment methods regarding uncertainty are precise, resulting in a well-founded opinion on the subject in question. Essential to such judgement is the application of rational thought. Colloquially, this might be termed 'good judgement.' An example of this process is demonstrated in the subsequent case study.

Case Study 34 – Accurate/Sound Judgement

Background:

The manager of a counter-terrorism team is tasked with identifying and recommending a new team leader. Two candidates are in contention.

Details:

Candidate A is a highly experienced team member who has occasionally acted as the team leader. This candidate has consistently received excellent appraisals and met key performance indicators. They are dedicated, committed to the team, and have a record of achieving exceptional results.

Candidate B, comparatively, has less experience. They have also acted as the team leader but received unfavourable appraisals and did not meet the key performance indicators. They have a history of underperformance and a poor work attitude.

Judgement

The manager evaluates both candidates against the job's key performance indicators, using these criteria to identify the most suitable candidate. Upon assessment, the manager determines that Candidate A has a stronger merit profile than Candidate B, forming the opinion (judgement) that Candidate A is the better choice. This judgement becomes the foundation for their recommendation (decision) to appoint Candidate A as the team leader.

11.2.2 Inaccurate/Unsound Judgement

An inaccurate judgement is as its name suggests: the decision-maker's cognitive assessment methods regarding an uncertainty are flawed. This results in a misguided opinion, which can lead to poor decisions. Such judgements might colloquially be termed 'poor judgement'. This process is exemplified in the case study below.

Case Study 35 – Inaccurate/Unsound Judgement

Context:

The situation mirrors that of the previous case study—the manager of a counter-terrorism team must identify and recommend a new team leader.

Detail:

The candidates' backgrounds remain as described previously. However, in this instance, the manager disregards each candidate's work history and adherence to key performance indicators. Instead, they solely trust the personal opinion of a colleague who had worked with both candidates over a decade ago. During that period, this colleague had a disagreement with Candidate A, which he did not disclose to the manager.

Judgement:

Based on the colleague's opinion, the manager forms the misguided opinion (judgement) that Candidate B is the superior choice. Consequently, without further research, the manager recommends (decides) Candidate B for the team leader position.

11.2.3 Impaired Judgement

Impaired judgement arises when the decision-maker is influenced by factors such as physical or psychological constraints, environmental conditions, excessive workload, bullying, substance influence, and more. These factors can inhibit their ability to correctly gauge and evaluate uncertainties. Consequently, such impediments can lead to unsound (or poor) judgements. In the counter-terrorism environment, many of these factors play a significant role in the decision-making process. An illustrative example of these factors affecting the decision-making process is delineated in the upcoming case study.

Case Study 36 – Impaired Judgement

Context:

The manager of a counter-terrorism team is tasked to identify and recommend a new team leader. There are twenty candidates.

Detail:

The team is short-staffed and managing 3 separate legitimate terrorist threats. The manager is required to formally report daily on each of these threats, which places a significant burden on their resources and time. Each candidate has submitted lengthy and complex applications accompanied by their respective CVs. The manager has been given a deadline to identify and recommend the preferred candidate. Failure to meet this deadline will result in the manager being reprimanded, which will be recorded in the manager's personnel file.

The manager's review and assessment of the candidates is compromised by competing priorities, workload, pressure, and time constraints.

Judgement:

Due to his impaired judgement, the manager fails to accurately assess the candidates, lacking the necessary time to appropriately evaluate each candidate and verify the details in their respective applications. Consequently, the manager mistakenly forms the opinion that a candidate who isn't suitable or qualified for the job is the preferred candidate.

11.2.4 Professional Judgement

Professional judgement, in the context of this book, is when an individual or group of experts who have demonstrated specialised:

- knowledge,
- training,
- experience, and
- technical expertise

in the field to which the uncertainty relates. These judgements are based on available evidence. The following case study illustrates professional judgement in the counter-terrorism environment.

136

Case Study 37 – Professional Judgement

Context:

A POI is nearing the end of their jail sentence for a terrorism offence and is placed before the courts for a determination of eligibility for a post-sentence detention scheme (preventative investigation).

Detail:

The court must determine whether the POI poses an unacceptable terrorism threat if they are released into the community at the conclusion of their sentence. The POI is a convicted terrorist, has shown no remorse during custody, and still adheres to an extreme interpretation of their belief, which includes the use of violence to further their belief.

The court seeks professional judgements from a variety of experts, including a psychologist, a parole officer, and a terrorism expert.

Judgement:

Each expert is provided an evidence package. Based on this evidence, their respective knowledge, training, experience, and technical expertise, each expert provides their judgements on whether or not the POI poses an unacceptable threat to the community and public safety.

Psychologist: Assesses the POI's psychological condition, their propensity to resort to violence, and comments on whether they still pose a threat to the community due to their vulnerability to violence (capability).

Parole Officer: The parole expert assesses whether the POI is compliant and amenable to adhering to any imposed conditions if released and whether their agency can successfully manage the POI if released on conditions of a post-sentence scheme (compliance).

Terrorism Expert: The terrorism expert comments on whether the POI is still radicalised or adheres to an extreme ideology that may pose a threat to the community (intent).

Result:

Based on the evidence, supplemented by the professional judgements of the experts, the court makes its independent determination (decision) on the post-sentence detention application.

11.2.5 Predictive Judgement (Anticipation)

Predictive judgements are another term for anticipation, which was addressed in the previous chapter. Anticipation is judgement of a future event occurring. Although this has been previously stated that prediction is an inappropriate term, predictive judgement is a term commonly used outside the counter-terrorism environment.

11.3 Factors that can Impact Judgement

Judgements are based on the individual's evaluation methods; they may be subjective or objective. While both methods can be impacted by various factors, it is the position of this book that subjective judgement methods are more susceptible to external influences like 'noise' and 'bias'. This book will focus on the concept of noise and its relationship and impact on judgements. (The concept of bias and its relationship and impact on decisions will be discussed in the next chapter).

11.3.1 Singular / Repetitive Judgements[44]

A judgement can either be singular – when a unique set of circumstances require a 'one-off' judgement – or repetitive – when judgements are made based on recurring or previously experienced circumstances.

Generally, the more frequently a judgement is made, the higher the likelihood of its accuracy. On the other hand, singular judgements, due to their unique nature, are more prone to inaccuracy. Familiarity with the circumstances increases the decision-maker's confidence, so judgements tend to become more accurate with experience.

11.3.2 Confidence

Confidence is crucial for decision-makers. It fosters trust in their judgements and subsequent decisions. A track record of accurate judgements and effective decisions enhances the decision-maker's

---

[44] Kahneman, D., Sibony, O., Sunstein, C.

confidence. While confidence is invaluable, it doesn't replace capability. Overconfidence, which can be seen in certain personality types or in environments where there have been repetitive successful outcomes, can lead to a lack of scrutiny. Decision-makers might then overestimate their judgement's accuracy, neglecting the need for regular review and recalibration of their cognitive assessments.

Overconfidence can culminate in poor judgements when the decision-maker disregards previous lessons learned. At times, it might even cause decision-makers to abandon their accepted methods of judgement, leading to what's colloquially referred to as a 'captain's call'. A captain's call epitomises a poor decision, generally stemming from an unsound judgement. An example of overconfidence leading to a 'captain's call' will be highlighted in the upcoming case study.

Case Study 38 – Over-Confidence (Captain's Call)

Background:

The decision-maker is a member of a management committee of a counter-terrorism team. The committee's role is to assess new information and determine whether it meets the criteria for an investigation by the team. On this occasion, the committee has received new information to assess. In brief, the information is that an identified POI poses a terrorist threat.

Detail:

The committee comprises senior members of the team who have jointly agreed on the criteria to accept an investigation. The decision-maker, having limited experience in this field, has only been involved in successful investigations. The details of the new information align with the criteria that would typically be accepted by the committee for an investigation.

Judgements

The decision-maker disregards the committee's advice and agreed protocols. Instead, they individually assess the information and determine that it doesn't meet the criteria for an investigation. Based on their own judgement (captain's call), they decide not to investigate the information and the POI.

139

Postscript

Twelve months later, the POI was apprehended by another counter-terrorism team while in the process of planning and preparing for a terrorist attack.

11.3.3 Noise

The judgement process may be subjective or objective. If the decision-maker's judgement process is subjective, it lends itself to a documented flaw called 'noise'[45]. Kahneman, Sibony, and Sunstein identified 'noise' as the myriad factors that cause discrepancies in individuals' judgements of the same set of facts. This flaw is exemplified by the variance in sentencing of offenders for identical offences or facts by different courts.

In the counter-terrorism environment, the impact of 'noise' is frequently observed in areas like threat and risk assessments, threat shifting, and determining suitable management strategies.

11.4 How to Improve Judgements

Despite being interrelated, judgements and decisions are distinct processes; accurate judgement can still result in a poor decision. This book posits that judgements, like other stages of the decision-making process, are cognitive skills that can be honed. Enhancing a decision-maker's judgement skills tips the balance in their favour, leading to sound decisions and better outcomes.

11.4.1 Aim of Judgements

The ultimate goal of a judgement is accuracy. Attaining accuracy necessitates the elimination of errors, which can hamper the precision of a decision-maker's judgements. To refine judgements, one must minimise these errors.

11.4.2 Knowledge and Experience

Terrorism, as a crime, possesses distinct characteristics. For judgements to be accurate, decision-makers must have an in-

---

[45] Kahneman, D., Sibony,O., Sunstein, C.

depth understanding of counter-terrorism principles. Without the appropriate specialised knowledge, a decision-maker might overlook or misinterpret a situation, adversely affecting their judgement. Extensive experience enhances the likelihood of making accurate judgements.

11.4.3 Subjective vs Objective

As mentioned, judgements can be rooted in either subjective or objective processes. Subjective judgements are error-prone and might be swayed by confidence, noise, and bias. Objective judgements, while less susceptible to these pitfalls, can still be problematic if their foundational models contain inherent flaws. Neither subjective nor objective processes are foolproof. This book suggests that judgements should favour objective processes wherever feasible. This not only reduces potential errors but also helps document the process — a vital step if subsequent decisions undergo external review.

11.4.4 Noise Audits

Kahneman, Sibony, and Sunstein state that noise and bias[46] create a variance in judgements. To mitigate the effects of noise and maintain consistency, they advocate for 'noise audits' in areas susceptible to noise. In the counter-terrorism domain, noise often influences the consistency of threat and risk assessments. It might be prudent to audit the organisation's threat and risk assessment processes to pinpoint and rectify factors causing discrepancies.

11.4.5 Diversity

Incorporating diverse perspectives can refine judgements. Decision-makers should enlist the expertise of others when making judgements. This not only heightens the chances of accuracy but also prevents 'group think'. The following case study illustrates the utility of diversity in judgements.

---

[46] Bias will be addressed in the following chapter on decision.

Case Study 39 – Diversity

Background:

The Senior Investigating Officer (SIO) of a counter-terrorism operation is contacted by an investigator who believes they have identified an additional terrorist cell member. The investigator seeks to include the new POI in the investigation's terms of reference. The SIO convenes a meeting with key team members to decide on the inclusion of the new POI.

Diversity:

The SIO gathers insights from senior team members:

Team Leader Cyber Operations: Indicates the POI frequently communicates with other cell members on covert social media platforms.

Team Leader Physical Surveillance: Notes the POI's frequent interactions with other cell members, including regular late-night visits to one member's residence.

Team Leader Electronic Surveillance: Discloses the POI uses a falsely registered mobile phone to liaise with other cell members.

Partner Agencies: Share intel suggesting the POI adheres to the same extreme interpretation of their beliefs as other cell members.

Judgement:

After weighing the evidence, the SIO opines there's a high probability the POI is an active member of the terrorist cell.

Decision:

The SIO resolves to include the POI in the investigation. This resolution takes effect when the terms of reference are updated to incorporate the POI.

11.4.6 Risk Intelligence[47]

A critical component of judgements is 'uncertainty'. Uncertainty arises when the results of potential outcomes from a judgement or decision are unknown. In the terrorism context, uncertainty is

---

[47] Evans, D.

linked to the threat. Generally, threats are managed by determining the likelihood of them materialising. The ability to estimate these uncertainties (threats/risks) accurately in the decision-making process is termed 'Risk Intelligence' (Risk Quotient - RQ).

Risk intelligence is integral to judgement. It can be defined as the ability to accurately estimate the probabilities of uncertainties (threats) occurring. Probabilities allow decision-makers to express their degree of belief (judgement) in relatively precise numerical terms.

This cognitive process occurs daily. For instance, each morning, an individual might estimate the uncertainty of that day's weather conditions (judgement). Based on this judgement, they choose appropriate attire (decision) best suited to the anticipated conditions.

Individuals skilled at accurately gauging the likelihood of uncertainties (threats) happening are deemed to possess high risk intelligence. Such individuals typically make more accurate judgements, viewing the world as it truly is. Conversely, those who struggle with this process likely possess lower risk intelligence and have a higher chance of making incorrect judgements.

Distinct from other intelligence measures like Intelligence Quotient (IQ) and Emotional Intelligence (EQ), Risk Intelligence (RQ) stands alone. Its level does not necessarily influence or correlate with other forms of intelligence.

Dylan Evans perceives risk intelligence as the balance between overconfidence and underconfidence. In contrast, David Apgar views it as the skill to form accurate judgements about specific new risks. For the purpose of this book, these risks might equate to threats.

Dylan Evans outlines four steps to consider when determining the accuracy of an uncertainty or, in this book's context, 'threat' through risk intelligence application:[48]

---

[48] ibid

1. Reflect on what you know about the uncertainty or threat.
2. Analyse each piece of information, determining its impact (probability) on your assessment.
3. Merging your existing knowledge with the new information should provide a cognitive estimation of the uncertainty/threat's outcome.
4. Convert this assessment into a numerical value representing your certainty degree (probability of the uncertainty/threat).

The rationale behind recommending a numerical representation of certainty in this book is its clear, precise nature, making it more user-friendly in assessing situations.

11.5 Summary

This book asserts that judgements and decisions, although interrelated, must be distinct to simplify and clarify the decision-making process. This separation aids in understanding the underlying concepts and enhancing judgement and decision-making abilities.

Judgement is a cognitive measurement of uncertainty applicable to both objective and subjective methods. It seeks to form an opinion supporting a corresponding decision. The primary goal, contingent on the situation, is to achieve accurate or sound judgements.

Judgements might be singular — unique, one-off evaluations based on unfamiliar circumstances. Alternatively, they could be repetitive, stemming from recurring or familiar scenarios. Typically, the more frequent a judgement, the more accurate it becomes. Conversely, singular judgements, being unique, often risk inaccuracy. Familiarity with the circumstances bolsters judgement confidence and precision, enhancing accuracy over time.

The judgement process is grounded in the individual's evaluation, achieved either subjectively or objectively. While both can be impacted by various factors, subjective methods are more susceptible to influences like 'noise' and 'bias'. In contrast, objective methods might suffer from inherent design flaws. This book suggests leaning towards objective methods where feasible.

The overarching aim is to achieve accurate judgements that lead to informed decisions, increasing the likelihood of favourable outcomes.

11.6 Key Points

- Judgements and decisions are interconnected, often overlapping during the decision-making process.
- Judgement is a cognitive uncertainty measure, applying to both objective and subjective methods, designed to shape an opinion supporting a related decision.
- The counter-terrorism realm recognises various judgement types: accurate/sound judgements; inaccurate/ unsound judgements; impaired judgements; professional judgements; and predictive judgements.
- Accurate judgements avoid bias and noise influences while maintaining suitable confidence levels.
- Judgements can be either singular or repetitive. The frequency of a judgement typically correlates with its accuracy.
- Judgements, as cognitive skills, can be enhanced by eliminating measurement errors, possessing in-depth subject knowledge, employing objective judgement support tools where possible, conducting noise audits, leveraging diversity, and applying risk intelligence principles.

12

Decisions

12.1 Introduction

An essential function for counter-terrorism professionals is to make good decisions in a time-poor, high-risk, dynamic environment. Decisions in this environment are held to a higher standard than those made in other areas. Decisions are a cognitive process to determine an action and its implementation. This can simply be referred to as making the choice (decision) and making it happen (implementation).

Decisions identify the optimal course of action when several alternatives are available, and their consequences cannot be forecast with any degree of certainty.[49] A good decision, whilst it considers uncertainty, makes a determination based on known facts. A decision is a subjective process influenced by a multitude of internal and external factors.

Given these fundamentals, this book posits that a good decision is a point-in-time determination based on available information, circumstances, knowledge, and experience. Once a decision has been made, it should be reassessed as new information becomes available or circumstances change. Decisions should be based on a sound rationale of known facts.

12.2 How Decisions Are Made

Decisions are a subjective process influenced by experience, emotions, procedures, circumstances, and knowledge. Like all cognitive skills, decisions can be improved through training and practice. An individual's psychology and personality significantly influence their decision-making process. Since every individual is

---

[49] Tryfos, P.

unique, their decision-making process is as well. The mechanics of decision-making are examined below from the perspective of several broad concepts.

12.2.1 'Fast' and 'Slow' Thinking

Daniel Kahneman identified two different systems of thinking when making decisions, 'Fast' thinking and 'Slow' thinking.[50] As their names suggest, fast thinking is based on quick thoughts and slow thinking is based on calculated or deliberate thoughts.

12.2.2 Fast Thinking

Fast thinking leads to immediate or snap decisions. Such decisions are made numerous times a day, for instance, crossing the road or switching checkout lines in a supermarket. Fast thinking is primarily relied upon during impromptu speeches, briefings, and presentations.

Typically, fast thinking results in reflex decisions made without deliberation. This type of thinking is essential for survival. The process of fast thinking can be influenced by several factors, such as:

Intuition

Fast-thinking decisions can be influenced by intuition, which stems from individual experiences, observations, and lessons learned. It's sometimes termed the *unknown knowns*. Counter-terrorism professionals might describe this as their 'gut feeling' or 'instinct'. Intuition is the internal force that might make one's hair stand on end when meeting someone for the first time, driven by past experiences that have unconsciously shaped one's knowledge.

Bias

All humans are subject to biases and prejudices. Factors such as race, gender, culture, brand allegiance, cognitive tendencies,

[50] Kahneman, D.

and organisational inclinations can unintentionally influence decisions. A decision based on a sentiment like 'he supports my team, so he must be okay' is an example of bias in decision-making.

Heuristics

Heuristics involve problem-solving based on self-educating techniques, using cognitive shortcuts to reach a decision. This may involve comparing the current issue with similar past experiences. Although this might seem like a lazy approach, it has its place, especially when needing an immediate decision amidst complex data. The phrases 'rule of thumb' and 'best-educated guess' exemplify this kind of thinking.

Selective Attention [51]

There's a limit to the amount of information an individual can process at a given time. Selective attention is the process where one focuses only on perceived important issues, neglecting what's deemed trivial. The challenge arises when focusing too intently on one matter, potentially overlooking others. This can result in impaired judgements, particularly when overwhelmed by vast amounts of information.

12.2.3 Positives/Negatives of Fast-Thinking Decisions[52]

Fast thinking is crucial for survival, allowing individuals to function without being bogged down by every decision. It facilitates multi-tasking and is an invaluable skill for briefings, presentations, media interviews, and public speaking.

However, from a decision-making perspective, it has its drawbacks. Fast thinking might be swayed by irrational thought, making the decision-making process susceptible to error. Generally, the faster the thinking, the more irrational influence on the decision, increasing the likelihood of mistakes.

---

[51] Cook, T.
[52] Kahneman, D.

Humans tend to seek the path of least resistance, especially under stress or when overwhelmed. A decision-maker who is fatigued and under pressure is prone to resort to fast-thinking decisions. This inclination is compounded when fast-thinking influences dominate the decision-making process more than slow-thinking considerations.

To avoid the pitfalls of fast thinking, individuals need to recognise that it is a cognitive process that can be improved with training and practice. To minimise the impact of these pitfalls, routines should be used that temporarily delay reflex decisions. The use of decision-making support tools will assist in slowing down the decision-making process.

12.2.4 Slow Thinking[53]

Slow thinking, also known as rational decision-making, is analytical and considerate. This type of thinking enables the application of greater thought by slowing down the process, allowing individuals to anticipate outcomes, assess their judgements, and consider their choices and how to implement them. Such thinking is often associated with major life decisions, like purchasing a car or a house. Slow thinking facilitates the use of decision-support tools and models, as well as the application of other forms of thinking such as critical thinking and reasoning.

Critical Thinking

There is no single definition for critical thinking. In the context of this book, it includes the ability to think clearly and rationally about an issue, enabling an accurate judgement and subsequent sound decision.

Arguments

When making decisions, it sometimes can be beneficial to distinguish between strong and weak arguments. In this context, these arguments can be seen as judgements. A strong argument

---

[53] Kahneman,D.

is both relevant and directly related to the issue, while a weak one is either not directly related or of minor importance to the issue.

Inferences

Every decision inherently has a degree of uncertainty; without uncertainty, there would be no decision. The intelligence collection capability might refer to this as an information gap. An inference is a judgement derived from observed or presumed facts. When making decisions, uncertainty is addressed by making probabilistic inferences from the available information. This requires a deliberate calculation or determination of the uncertainty. An inference provides an explanation, and is NOT a fact. For instance, if you turn the light switch to 'on' and the room remains dark, you might infer that the light bulb is broken. The decision would be to replace the bulb.

12.2.5 Positives and Negatives of Slow-Thinking Decisions

Slow-thinking decisions are a deliberate process aimed at a sound, rational outcome. They demand time and effort, and can be challenging in high-stress, time-poor environments. It's unrealistic to expect decision-makers to make major snap decisions in high-risk situations without proper consideration and still expect positive outcomes. In such cases, favourable outcomes would likely result more from luck than skill. While slow thinking promotes sound decisions, all decisions come with some uncertainty or risk. This unknown factor might still lead to negative outcomes, regardless of the decision's quality.

12.2.6 Reasoning

Reasoning is another form of thinking when making decisions. It is a series of cognitive processes that transform information into conclusions and judgements, supporting the final decision by pinpointing the best course of action. Primarily, there are two major forms of reasoning: deductive and inductive.

Deductive Reasoning

This employs top-down logic based on premises leading to a conclusion. If the premises are accurate, then the conclusion will be too. Example: All birds have feathers. All swans are birds. Hence, all swans have feathers.

Inductive Reasoning

Inductive reasoning uses bottom-up logic. The conclusion might be accurate and have some support, but the reasoning could still be flawed. Example: Most bushfires originate from the west; I can detect the scent of a bushfire. This bushfire must be coming from the west.

12.2.7 Problem Solving

Viewing the decision as a problem, creates an alternate form of thinking. Problem solving is both a creative and analytical process involving the identification of a problem, establishing its cause, and pinpointing numerous potential solutions. Judgement assesses the identified solutions. The decision is the selection of the best solution and the means of its implementation. The ultimate goal of counter-terrorism is to solve an ongoing issue.

12.3 Factors Affecting Decisions

Decisions can be influenced by various internal and external factors, including cognitive, socioeconomic, environmental, and organisational influences.

12.3.1 Situational Awareness[54]

In this context, situational awareness refers to the operational environment and its effect on the decision-making process. Every operational decision must account for events happening in and around an incident's vicinity. In a counter-terrorism context, this refers to global events. Situational awareness helps to understand circumstances while considering potential repercussions. It assists

---

[54] Cook, T.

in averting poor judgements and decisions and counters narrow-mindedness and groupthink.

12.3.2 Policy and Procedure

Organisations establish policies and procedures to ensure consistent decisions by their employees. In certain situations, these policies might remove the decision-making aspect from the operational equation. An Australian law enforcement example of this scenario is illustrated in the following case study:

Case Study 40 – Policy or Decision?

Circumstance:

The commander plans the arrest of an offender accused of killing a police officer. Part of the arrest procedure involves executing a search warrant at the offender's residence. The offender, known for violence, especially against police, reportedly has firearms and intends to use them against officers if approached. The risk rating for this operation is 'high'. (Any risk rating at high has a mandatory requirement for the deployment of tactical police).

Action:

Deploy specialised tactical police units to make the arrest and enter the premises to execute the search warrant.

Question:

Is this a product of decision-making or simply following a policy?

12.3.3 Framing

Framing refers to the position or perspective of the decision-maker on the relevant issue. The framing or decision-maker's perspective can be influenced by how the issue is presented. This is illustrated in the Maslow's Hammer scenario, an example of a cognitive bias. Maslow stated, 'I suppose it is tempting, if the only tool you have is a hammer, to treat everything as if it were a nail'. In a modern-day setting, another example of framing might occur when an HR manager investigates a complaint about an argument between two colleagues at the staff Christmas party where alcohol was served. The HR manager's initial framing might be that both parties, rightly or wrongly, were intoxicated.

12.3.4 Other Factors

Other factors that may impact the decision-making process include assumption of absolutes, fallacy (worst-case scenario), imagination, the burden of others' expectations, cognitive biases such as anchoring, memory, errors, intelligence, and optimal thinking.

12.4 Judgement / Decision Support Tools

Decision support tools or models provide rational, measurable, and/ or scientific analysis to the decision-making process. These tools can support judgements and/or help in determining and actioning the optimal alternative. Such tools represent slow thinking applied to decision-making. The most common decision support tool used by many Australian organisations is risk rating matrices. Examples of other decision support tools/models and their shortcomings within the counter-terrorism environment are provided below.

12.4.1 Pro/Con List

A common initial decision support model is the 'pro-con list'. This process involves creating lists of positive outcomes (pros) and comparing them against the negative outcomes (cons).

Shortcomings:

- Assumes there are only two options
- Limits exploration of alternatives
- Reduces problem-solving capabilities
- Considers all items, whether 'pro' or 'con', as having equal weight
- Views each item as independent, though some may be interrelated
- Due to human bias, often identifies more 'pros' than 'cons' (believing the grass is always greener).

12.4.2 Weighing the Costs and Benefits

This model extends the 'pro-con list'. Here, the variables are assigned a value, and the resulting score informs the decision. Scoring in this manner addresses some of the limitations of the pro-con list and facilitates the comparison of multiple options while accounting for interconnected items.

Shortcomings:

- Assigning value is subjective and prone to bias
- Potential for errors in determining values
- Temptation to adjust values to achieve a pre-determined outcome
- Difficult to quantify intangible items
- Can be time-consuming.

12.4.3 Decision Tree

The decision tree is a diagram that uses branches to examine decision points. The leaves represent different possible outcomes, giving the diagram a tree-like appearance. This approach helps analyse decisions with uncertain outcomes.

Shortcomings:

- Generally applies probability to outcomes
- The number of variables is a subjective assessment
- Becomes complicated when dealing with multiple options
- Doesn't account for 'black swans'
- Difficult to apply to the counter-terrorism environment

12.4.4 Paired Comparison Analysis

This model relies on underlying priorities to base decisions. It is applicable when there are several complex issues to consider. It generally uses a chart where it lists the required decisions together with every possible option. The process involves comparing all decisions and their options directly against one another to determine the optimal course of action.

Shortcomings:

- Difficult to apply to the counter-terrorism environment
- Subjective in nature
- The process is complex
- Time-consuming
- Difficult to ensure it addresses the context of the proposed decision

12.4.5 Decision Logs

A decision log is a process of recording a decision, its context, and other relevant information contemporaneously, which includes the rationale and judgements. Decision logs enable the decision-maker to incorporate other factors like personal experiences, beliefs, and potential biases. Decision logs can be made in real-time or as soon as feasible post-event. They can be referenced when the decision is being scrutinised by independent entities like internal reviews or independent commissions of inquiry.

Decision logs are apt for the counter-terrorism environment. It's the stance of this book that decision logs, at a minimum, should be employed when making crucial and/or significant decisions.

Shortcomings:

- Necessitates discipline to complete
- Rationale must be penned before making the decision; otherwise, it can be manipulated to justify a preconceived decision
- During periods of high operational tempo, decision logs can be challenging to fill out due to competing priorities.

Figure 12.1 below furnishes an example of a decision log template:

Figure 12.1: Decision Log Template

Decision Log
Activity:

Context:

Rationale (include judgements):

Decision:

Implementation:
Signature:

Time / Date:

12.5 Instructions (How to Complete a Decision Log)

Ideally, decision logs are filled out contemporaneously or as soon after the event as possible. This ensures their reliability from an evidentiary standpoint if third parties need to review the decision. The decision-maker themselves or an assistant, colloquially termed a 'scribe', may complete them. These decisions can be recorded via video, audio, electronically, or in written form.

Generally, each log captures one decision. Hence, if there are two decisions, two separate logs are needed. The decision is made after documenting the context and rationale. In essence, the decision should follow the sequence of the Decision Log Template presented above in Figure 12.1. The log usually starts with the activity's name to distinguish it from other terrorism operations or activities.

12.5.1 Context

Context describes the reason for making the decision at a particular time. For instance, a decision might be necessary regarding resource deployment due to a shift in circumstances. Clarifying this situation provides context for the ensuing rationale and decision.

12.5.2 Rationale

Rationale encompasses all factors potentially influencing the decision. It offers a platform for the decision-maker to enumerate all relevant details that might (or might not) sway their decision at that juncture. This includes known facts, assumptions, past experiences, knowledge, judgements, inferences, alternatives, assessments, and beliefs. It can also cover external or internal pressures impacting the decision-maker, along with the recognition of any biases.

12.5.3 Decision

Decision pertains to the chosen course of action and its execution. It should be formulated only after finalising the context and rationale. Making a decision out of sequence may tempt the decision-maker to adjust their rationale to align with a preordained decision.

12.5.4 Implementation

This includes all strategies and taskings required to be undertaken in order to enable the decision to be executed to the decision-maker's expectation.

12.5.5 Completing the Log

The log concludes with the time and date of completion and the identification of the individual responsible for the decision. These particulars authenticate the decision and its accompanying documentation and might help ascertain its evidentiary value in the future.

12.6 Risk Appetite

Another component impacting decisions is the concept of *risk appetite*. This represents the level of risk an individual or organisation is willing to accept due to potential consequences stemming from their decisions. While it's related to the concept of 'risk tolerance', both together determine the boundaries of acceptable risk.

The product of these boundaries establishes a risk level, prompting the individual or organisation to deploy mitigation or management strategies for that threat/risk. An individual's risk appetite can vary depending on several subjective factors, including: consequence, personality, experience, exposure, work ethic, competence, and burden of expectation.

For an organisation, risk appetite might generally be objective, influenced by factors such as: history, level of exposure, consequence, policy, corporate responsibilities, legislative requirements, and community/board expectations.

12.6.1 Risk Appetite and Productivity

An individual's or organisation's risk appetite can be 'low', 'neutral', or 'high'. There's a correlation between risk appetite and productivity. Individuals or entities with a high risk appetite typically demonstrate higher productivity but assume greater risks. From an organisational standpoint, decision-makers with a high risk appetite might achieve superior outcomes but expose the organisation to higher liability levels.

A case in point is the 2017 Royal Commission into Misconduct in the Banking, Superannuation, and Financial Services Industry in Australia, which showcased the repercussions for organisations that prioritise high-risk decisions for maximum gain, sidelining ethical considerations.

On the other hand, those with low or neutral risk appetites exhibit lower productivity, achieving fewer results but incurring reduced risks. While these decision-makers play it safe, they often limit the organisation's growth potential. The goal is to strike a balance in risk appetite that encourages ethical outcomes while curbing potential risks and exposures. This equilibrium, as Dylan Evans noted, is the 'golden mean'.

12.7 Summary

It's vital for counter-terrorism professionals to make sound decisions in fast-paced, high-risk, dynamic environments. Decisions represent a cognitive process that dictates action and its implementation, which can be succinctly described as making the choice (decision) and executing it (implementation).

Good decisions, despite uncertainty, are grounded in known facts. The decision-making process is subjective, influenced by a myriad of internal and external factors. Every individual's decision-making mechanism is distinct but is primarily driven by two systems: 'Fast' thinking and 'Slow' thinking.[55] As implied by their labels, fast thinking relies on instinctive judgments, while slow thinking involves deliberate, calculated thought.

Factors influencing fast thinking include intuition, bias, heuristics, and selective attention. Necessary for survival, fast thinking facilitates multitasking and is pivotal for briefings, presentations, and public speaking. A major downside of fast thinking is its susceptibility to irrationality, making decisions prone to mistakes. Generally, the faster the decision-making process, the more irrationality impacts the outcome, increasing the potential for errors.

Conversely, slow thinking represents rational decision-making. It's analytical and deliberate, permitting the individual to foresee outcomes, evaluate their judgments, consider options, and strategise their implementation. Typically linked with major life decisions like buying a car or home, slow thinking encourages the employment of decision-support tools and methods, integrating other cognitive processes like critical thinking, arguments, inferences, and reasoning.

Decisions can be swayed by an array of cognitive, socioeconomic, environmental, and organisational elements. Other influences encompass situational awareness, policies, and

---

[55] Kahneman, D.

framing, which defines the lens through which the decision-maker perceives the issue. Tools or models that offer rational, measurable outcomes can support decisions, representing slow thinking's application. This book explored several such tools, identifying contemporary decision logs as the most fitting in this environment.

12.8 Key Points

- For counter-terrorism professionals and decision-makers, it's essential to make informed decisions in a time-poor, high-risk, and dynamic environment.
- Decisions made in this environment are held to a higher standard than those made in other areas.
- Decisions are a cognitive process determining an action and its subsequent implementation.
- They discern the best course of action when multiple alternatives are available and their consequences cannot be precisely predicted.[56]
- A quality decision, even amid uncertainty, arrives at a conclusion based on established facts.
- A good decision is a determination made at a specific moment, considering the information, circumstances, knowledge, and experience at hand. Decisions should be revisited as new information arises or situations evolve.
- Decisions, like all cognitive skills, are subjective, influenced by experience, emotions, procedures, circumstances, and knowledge. They can be honed through training and practice.
- This book highlights two systems of thinking in decision-making: 'Fast' thinking and 'Slow' thinking.[57] Fast thinking is instinctive, whereas slow thinking is more deliberate and calculated.
- Fast thinking facilitates immediate decisions essential for survival but is more susceptible to errors.

---

[56] Tryfos, P.
[57] Kahneman, D.

- Slow thinking, in contrast, is analytical and methodical, typically associated with life's more significant decisions. This guide advocates for the use of slow thinking whenever possible, as it fosters superior decisions.
- Decision support tools epitomise slow thinking. This book found that contemporary decision logs are the most appropriate decision support tool for this context.
- Despite uncertainty, quality decisions don't always lead to the desired outcomes.
- Though every individual can make decisions, leaders are expected to make superior choices compared to their subordinates.

13

Implementation

13.1 Introduction

In this books context, *implementation* refers to the strategies used to execute a decision. A decision and its execution are intertwined; one cannot exist without the other. While it concludes the decision-making process, effective implementation is crucial to optimising the outcomes of a decision. One could argue that implementation is the act of executing a chosen option from multiple alternatives. In relation to *Part B: The Decision-Making Process*, we will delve into its application within the counter-terrorism management continuum.

13.2 Implementation Gap

Once a decision is made, it is vital to convert that choice into effective action within an appropriate timeframe to enhance the likelihood of a good outcome and/or meet expectations. Failure to effectively implement the decision in a timely manner may result in an 'implementation gap.'[58] The implementation gap is where the results of the action turn out differently from what was decided. To be successful, the implementation process must achieve the anticipated results. If it doesn't meet the anticipated outcome, it may be referred to as an implementation failure. An example of an implementation failure is set out below in the study, implementation failure – NDIS.

Case Study 41 – Implementation Failure - NDIS

Circumstance:

In 2009, the Australian Productivity Commission estimated that approximately 410,000 Australians were suffering from significant and on-going disabilities requiring long-term care and support. At this time,

---

[58] Campos, Vivacqua and Borges 2010.

Australian Governments (State/Commonwealth) supported people with disabilities and their careers and families through the National Disability Agreement (NDA). It was recognised that the NDA wasn't adequately addressing the needs of those suffering from disabilities, signalling a need for reform.

Decision:

To rectify this, the decision to initiate a new program named the National Disability Insurance Scheme (NDIS) was made. This program would aid people with chronic, significant disabilities. In 2011, The Productivity Commission projected that the NDIS would necessitate an additional $6.5 billion annually, coupled with the then-current disability support budget of $7.5 billion per year. The total NDIS funding was pegged at $14 billion annually. One objective of the NDIS was cost-effectiveness.

Implementation:

In March 2013, almost two years post-decision, *The National Disability Insurance Scheme Act 2013* was enacted. On 1 July 2013, the NDIS commenced in stages, beginning with a pilot and then a full rollout from July 2016. The scale and complicated nature of the NDIS meant that there have been some challenges to its implementation. These include:[59]

- information and technology problems;
- development of adequate support programs;
- market readiness; and
- workforce capacity.

However, the two most significant implementation failures in the NDIS where the outcomes haven't met the anticipated results have been in:

- funding; and
- prevalence of fraud.

The costs for the NDIS in 2023 is estimated at $35 billion and is estimated to rise to approximately $45 billion by 2025.[60] In relation to the prevalence of fraud, October 2022 the Australian Government identified over $300 million in suspected fraudulent payments that will require an additional investment of $48 million in an attempt to reduce its occurrence.

The NDIS demonstrates how a good decision which isn't effectively implemented (gap) can result in an implementation failure.

---

[59] Parliament of Australia (2018)

[60] Clun, R. (2022) The $60 billion question: How to fund and run the NDIS (SMH)

13.3 How to Avoid Implementation Gaps

Implementation often involves a series of interconnected decisions followed by respective actions. The objective is to sidestep gaps that could lead to failures. Some common factors contributing to implementation gaps are outlined below in the 'Common Causes of Implementation Gaps Toolbox.'

Figure 13.1: Common Causes of Implementation Gaps Toolbox

Factors
Common Causes Implementation Gaps

Factors (right column):
- Poor decisions
- Miscommunication
- Inadequate tasking
- Cultural barriers
- Insufficient planning
- Lack of capability
- Insufficient capacity
- Weak leadership
- Misidentifying the root cause/s,
- Failure to get 'buy in' from all involved parties
- Inadequate monitoring
- Neglecting to review

13.4 Implementation of the Counter-Terrorism Management Continuum

Management continuum is a comprehensive term for all strategies derived from the decision-making process and applied to address a terrorist threat. Depending on the nature of the threat, a decision determines the best course of action to counteract it. It is anticipated that the chosen strategy will be executed to the decision-maker's expectations.

For instance, if the manager of a shopping centre (a location that attracts large gatherings) is alerted to a potential terrorist threat, the decision, informed by the management continuum, might be to enhance CCTV coverage (electronic surveillance) throughout the premises. While the decision-maker might not be responsible for physically installing the cameras, they would expect them to satisfy the requirements of the security team overseeing the surveillance. In this scenario, the decision-maker must devise a comprehensive plan to ensure optimal camera placement and coverage, while also ensuring adequate resources and competent installation. The decision-maker should also monitor the installation's progress, ensuring that the security team is engaged and understands the importance of the enhanced surveillance in countering the potential threat, ensuring buy in. Any oversight in these areas could lead to an implementation gap, potentially failing to detect and neutralise the threat. The concept of the management continuum is illustrated in Diagram 13.1.

Diagram 13.1

THE MANAGEMENT CONTINUUM OF THE LIFE CYCLE OF A RADICALISED EXTREMIST

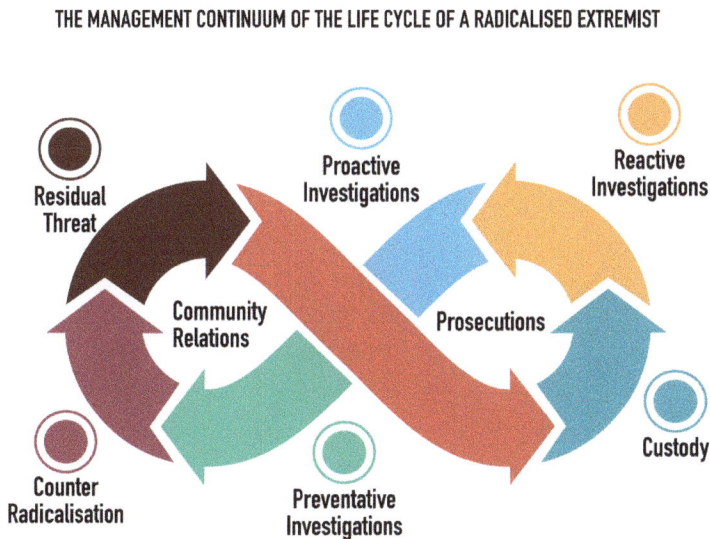

It is acknowledged that the implementation process includes further decisions and subsequent implementations. The decision-making process is a complicated series of steps that continually overlap one another throughout the process.

14

Psychological Health

14.1 Introduction

Counter-terrorism represents a challenging environment, prolonged exposure can adversely impact an individual's physical and psychological health. One might assume that, given this nature, the psychological welfare of employees would be a top priority for organisations involved in counter-terrorism. However, in 2022 the Interim Report by the Royal Commission into Defence and Veteran Suicide, identified over 50 previous reports and more than 750 recommendations on the topics of suicide, suicidality and psychological wellbeing of serving and ex-serving members of Australian Defence Force (ADF), noting the limited response from Australian Governments and the ADF in endeavouring to resolve these issues. Putting these tragic circumstances into perspective, this report found that women who served in the ADF were twice as likely to die from suicide than those who had not. From a policing perspective, a number of Australian Police Associations have reported a dramatic increase in experienced officers leaving the force through either injury (including psychological) or taking early retirement due to stress. Both the ADF and Police are leading counter-terrorism organisations, these issues underscore a significant gap in the leadership of these organisations understanding the origins and effective management of psychological health.

To help elucidate these complex issues, this book will employ a football analogy, shedding light from a practitioner's viewpoint on managing colleagues' mental health. In football, as in any contact sport, players may sustain injuries. The objective for the team manager is to reduce these injuries, ensuring the best team plays. If a manager observes a player struggling on the field, they may, to avert potential injury, substitute that player and send them for a medical assessment. Here, the manager relies on their expertise, observations, and the game's conditions to judge whether an injury has occurred, and if so, to act swiftly to mitigate its severity.

Professionals in counter-terrorism, similar to athletes in contact sports, don't get injured every time they're exposed to their work. However, the longer their exposure, the higher the risk of injury. In a psychological context, early identification of symptoms is crucial to preventing potential harm.

Although I am not a medical expert, this chapter draws from my experiences and insights as a seasoned counter-terrorism professional who has encountered psychological challenges in this demanding environment. This chapter's aim is to spotlight various issues and common pitfalls affecting colleagues' psychological health, grounded on the principle:

Psychological Health Principle

Only suitably qualified medical professionals can diagnose and treat a psychological injury.

14.2 Psychological Injury

Psychological injury is defined by Safe Work Australia as '…a range of cognitive, emotional, and behavioural symptoms that interfere with a worker's life and can significantly affect how they feel, think, behave, and interact with others.'[61] It can occur after repeated and ongoing exposure to potentially traumatic events, loss, and extreme stress.[62] Psychological injury can encompass conditions such as:

- depression;
- anxiety;
- social phobia disorders;
- obsessive compulsive disorders;
- panic disorders; and
- post-traumatic stress disorder (PTSD);

---

[61] Safe Work Australia
[62] Papazoglou, K., Tuttle, B.

Each condition has distinct symptoms or indicators. An individual might grapple with multiple conditions at once, underscoring the point that counter-terrorism professionals and decision-makers are not equipped to diagnose them.

14.3 Trauma

Trauma can be multifaceted, spanning from physical to emotional dimensions. This chapter emphasises emotional trauma, which can be defined as an emotional reaction to a significant event or situation that inflicts physical or emotional harm, or creates feelings of threat or unsafety.[63] Traumatic experiences might be singular or recurrent over an extended timeframe.

Emotional trauma can manifest directly or indirectly. Direct trauma pertains to firsthand experiences, like an Ambulance Officer attending a fatal car crash scene. Conversely, indirect trauma relates to the emotional effects stemming from hearing others' traumatic experiences, commonly experienced by service providers, social workers, healthcare practitioners, and family members. Terms such as *vicarious trauma* or *secondary traumatic stress* can describe indirect trauma. It often emerges from cumulative exposure to others' trauma, leading to empathic distress.

Both emotional and physical manifestations can stem from trauma, interfering with an individual's professional performance or daily life. Both direct and indirect trauma types are pervasive in counter-terrorism environments, as illustrated in the subsequent case study titled 'Examples of Direct and Indirect Trauma in Counter-Terrorism'.

---

[63] American Psychological Association

Case Study 42 –

Examples of Direct and Indirect Trauma in Counter-Terrorism

Examples of Direct Trauma:

Examples of direct trauma experienced in the Australian counter-terrorism environment include:

- CT professionals attending the shooting of Omar Badajam in the 2005 Operation Pendennis/Eden.
- CT investigators tasked to view and catalogue evidence from over 900 million pages of extremist material, including beheading-style videos, Operation Pendennis.
- CT professionals attending the shooting of Numan Haidar, Endeavour Hills.
- CT professionals attending the Lindt Café siege.
- CT professionals attending the shooting of Curtis Cheng.
- CT professionals attending the 2016 Minto stabbing.
- CT professionals attending the Queanbeyan stabbing attacks in 2017.
- CT professionals attending the Brighton siege in 2017.
- CT professionals attending the Bourke Street stabbing attack by Hassan Shire Ali.
- CT professionals conducting online engagement.
- CT professionals subject to threats or terrorist attacks.

Examples of Indirect Trauma:

Indirect trauma experienced in the Australian counter-terrorism environment includes:

- CT professionals engaged in family liaison.
- CT professionals interviewing victims of terrorism.
- CT professionals managing 'at-risk' POIs (HRTO/THRO).
- CT professionals investigating and/or analysing the above examples of direct trauma.
- CT professionals engaged in various legal aspects, from both defence and prosecution perspectives.
- CT professionals involved in custody processes.
- CT professionals involved in assessing threat/risk, training, and research.
- Family members of CT professionals exposed to trauma.

14.4 Stress

Stress is considered the body's response to circumstances. It can be positive, enhancing productivity, or negative when excessive, thereby impeding productivity or harming an individual's psychological wellbeing. There's a direct correlation between pressure and stress: the greater the pressure on an individual or organisation, the higher the stress level.

Excessive exposure to stress might lead an individual to experience emotional and mental exhaustion or what's commonly termed as *burnout*. Burnout results from severe, prolonged stress, leaving the individual feeling exhausted and unable to cope.

14.5 Anxiety

Anxiety is a behavioural response in anticipation of future events. It varies among individuals. Distinct from *fear*, anxiety might manifest as worry, nervousness, apprehension, or dread. While a natural response to stress and pressure, excessive or chronic anxiety can be harmful to an individual's physical and psychological wellbeing.

14.6 Psychological and Physical Injury

Emotions and cognitive processes trigger physiological responses. The more intense these processes, the stronger the physiological response. Chronic and excessive responses can negatively affect an individual's physical wellbeing.

14.7 Possible Symptoms (Indicators) of Psychological Injury[64]

Individuals experience psychological injuries differently. The manifestation of symptoms in counter-terrorism professionals or decision-makers, indicating potential psychological injury, varies. Below are indicators of potential physical/behavioural and emotional/cognitive psychological injuries:

---

[64] These are not exhaustive lists. The presence of a number of these indicators is not necessarily proof that the individual is suffering from a psychological injury, but rather it provides an indication which may require further consideration.

Figure 14.1: Behavioural/Physical Indicators (Potential Psychological Injury) Tool Box

Injury	Potential Physical/Behavioural Indicators
Psychological	• Change in physical appearance. • Decline in physical health. • Altered eating/sleeping patterns. • Increased alcohol consumption. • Substance abuse. • Engaging in risky behaviour. • Loss of attention. • Mood swings. • Irrational behaviours. • Fatigue. • Decrease in productivity. • Pervading negativity. • Frequent absenteeism. • Verbal expressions of suffering ('leakage'). • Social isolation/avoidance. • Visible distress. • Hyper-vigilance. • Displays of shame, guilt, anger, frustration, or depression. • Experiencing headaches, heartburn, rashes or general unwellness. • Loss of sense of humour. • Displays of violence.

Figure 14.2: Emotional/Cognitive Indicators (Potential Psychological Injury) Tool Box

Set out below is an Indicators of Potential Emotional/Cognitive Behavioural Indicators Psychological Injury Toolbox which provides a list of some of the potential symptoms:

Injury	Potential Emotional/Cognitive Indicators
Psychological	<ul><li>Changes in emotional state.</li><li>Inability to concentrate.</li><li>Feeling of numbness.</li><li>Prolonged anxiety.</li><li>Feelings of hopelessness.</li><li>Increase in risk-taking.</li><li>Loss of cognitive ability.</li><li>Memory issues.</li><li>Feeling depressed.</li><li>Pervading negativity.</li><li>Loss of energy/exhaustion.</li><li>Feeling distressed.</li><li>Loss of enjoyment.</li><li>Difficulty making decisions.</li><li>Feelings of shame, guilt, anger, frustration.</li><li>Emotional detachment.</li></ul>

14.7.1 Significance of Observing these Potential Indicators

The early identification of such indicators and appropriate responses by management or colleagues is essential for ensuring an individual's psychological wellbeing. It's common for managers to observe these potential indicators and misidentify them as signs of other issues, like poor work performance. For instance, mistaking poor performance as the problem instead of recognising it as a symptom of a psychological injury can lead to unjust punitive actions against the individual.

Misinterpreting these indicators can aggravate the individual, further impacting their wellbeing. These situations can lead to what's termed a *moral injury*. A case study illustrating this scenario is provided below.

Case Study 43 – Incorrectly Assessing a Psychological Health

Circumstance:

During the COVID-19 pandemic, an Australian police jurisdiction set up an Operations Centre to steer their response. Due to the significance of these duties, only officers recognised as highly capable and competent were chosen and seconded to the Operations Centre.

The strain on police resources during the pandemic meant that each officer in the Operations Centre had to manage their daily duties from their original Command in addition to their new roles. Effectively, this doubled their workload.

However, their duties at the Operations Centre always took precedence. This lack of support for these officers was exacerbated when those seconded from already busy Commands weren't given due consideration. One seconded officer, considered an expert in their field, began to show signs of psychological stress due to the overwhelming responsibilities.

Action:

Instead of addressing this as a workload and/or health issue, it was treated as a performance problem. The officer faced formal disciplinary action, adding to their existing stress. Feeling isolated and betrayed, the officer's psychological health declined, ultimately requiring professional medical intervention. This mismanagement was never acknowledged by the officer's superiors or organisation.

14.8 Moral Injury

Moral injury is an emerging area of research. The term itself was first coined by Jonathon Shay in 1994 whilst examining the aftermath of the Vietnam War on its veterans. He defined this term as '...a betrayal of what's right, by someone who holds legitimate authority, in a high-stakes situation.'[65] In 2009, Brett Litz, Nathan Stein and Eileen Delaney and others added to this growing body of research by defining it as '...the lasting psychological, biological, spiritual, behavioural and social impact of perpetrating, failing to prevent, bearing witness to, or learning about acts that transgress deeply held moral beliefs and expectations'[66] Research suggests that this issue is prevalent in military, first responders and the emergency services.

While the name suggests an injury, this book views 'moral injury' more as direct emotional trauma rather than a clinically diagnosed injury. In essence, moral injury (trauma) can contribute to, or cause, a psychological injury.

A moral injury (trauma) can occur when the individual is engaged or witnesses' activity that is contrary to the individual's moral beliefs. It is a subjective process and the violation of the individual's moral values may lead to feelings of anger, guilt, shame and self-doubt.[67] It may also lead to feelings of distress, distrust, depression, isolation, and vulnerability to self-harm.[68]

This trauma can stem from perceived betrayals — be it intentional harm by colleagues, leaders, organisations, or governments.[69] It can also emerge from witnessing or participating in traumatic events, unfair actions, corruption, or cruelty. In a high-stakes environment like counter-terrorism, many scenarios can trigger this condition, including the malicious shifting of

---

[65] Shay, J.
[66] Litz, B. T., Stein, N., Delaney, E. et al.
[67] Jinkerson, J. D.
[68] Jamieson, N.
[69] ibid

threat from one organisation to another or imposing of unrealistic bureaucratic barriers. From an organisational standpoint, poor management, inadequate leadership, or bad decisions can all lead to this form of trauma.

14.9 Counter-Terrorism Environment

Counter-terrorism presents several factors that distinguish it as both unique and hostile. Owing to these unique challenges, it necessitates specific policies to support the psychological well-being of its professionals. This section will explore these unique factors from both trauma and stress perspectives.

14.9.1 Vicarious Trauma

Within this environment, individuals experience indirect emotional trauma (vicarious) through exposure to victims. The inherent nature of terrorism guarantees the presence of victims or intended victims. Every counter-terrorism operation, be it preventative, proactive, or reactive, involves victims that professionals and decision-makers must address.

The scope for defining victims in terrorism is broader than in traditional crimes. A larger victim pool means increased exposure to vicarious trauma. In this context, victims can encompass:

- actual victims of the terrorist act;
- perceived victims of the terrorist act;
- targeted group of the terrorist act (including intended acts)
- families of these victims;
- witnesses to the terrorists' acts (traumatic incidents);
- families of the terrorists;
- first responders; and
- counter-terrorism professionals.

The extended parameters of victims resulting from terrorism is illustrated in the below case study Lindt Café victims.

Case Study 44 – Lindt Café Siege Victims.

Circumstances:

On 15 December 2014, Man Monis, armed with a sawn-off shotgun and a backpack he claimed contained explosives, took several hostages at the Lindt café in Sydney. He displayed a black flag with Arabic writing, known as the 'Shahada'. Monis indirectly communicated with the police through his hostages, claiming he represented the Islamic State (IS). The siege concluded in the early hours of 16 December 2014, culminating in the death of Monis and two innocent hostages.

Victims:

Traditionally, the two deceased and the surviving hostages would be considered the primary victims of this crime. However, in the context of terrorism, a broader range of individuals significantly impacted by this event would be considered victims, including:

- family and friends of innocent victims;
- family and friends of hostages;
- witnesses and bystanders to the siege;
- Sydney Council officers required to manage the city infrastructure during the siege;
- Uniformed police and ambulance officers that were the first responders to the siege;
- negotiators;
- tactical police and emergency personnel that entered the café to save lives and render the scene safe;
- counter-terrorism practitioners and decision-makers engaged in the operation; and
- innocent family and friends of Monis.

14.9.2 Threat (Direct/Indirect Trauma)

This book defines 'threat' as the intent to cause harm, damage, or injury to another or others. Such threats can be 'actual' or 'perceived'. It's well documented, both in Australia and abroad, that counter-terrorism professionals and decision-makers are often targeted by terrorists, including their family, friends, and colleagues. Irrespective of cultural or societal differences, counter-terrorism professionals are frequently within the groups targeted by terrorists.

This constant exposure is also endless; even if a person of interest (POI) is imprisoned or abroad, they still represent a credible threat. The threat posed by a POI situated overseas but considered a genuine threat in Australia is depicted in the following case study.

Case Study 45 – Off-Shore Threat

Circumstances:

During the Syrian conflict after the Arab Spring, Australian authorities estimated that over a hundred Australian citizens and residents joined hostilities with terrorist groups like the Islamic State (IS), often referred to as 'foreign fighters'.

Exposure:

Australian journalists often covered the activities of these Australian foreign fighters. On one occasion, a report by an Australian journalist offended one of the foreign fighters in Syria. This led the fighter to threaten the journalist via social media, eventually inciting local extremists in Australia to target the journalist. Whilst the foreign fighter was subsequently killed in action, up until that point, it was believed that he had the intent and resources in Australia to orchestrate an attack on the journalist.

14.9.3 Violence (Physical/Emotional Trauma)

Violence is the currency of terrorism. The more violent the act, the more publicity and influence it garners. It's fair to say that no terrorist act happens without the threat of violence. Assessing a Person of Interest's (POI) intention and capability for violence is critical for counter-terrorism professionals when determining appropriate mitigation strategies.

14.9.4 Heavy Workload (Stress)

Like all business activities, counter-terrorism efforts ebb and flow. But during times of direct threats, religious celebrations, anniversaries with symbolic significance, or in response to global events, operational tempo can surge to extremely high levels. Increased workload and/or threats amplify the pressure on professionals and decision-makers, directly correlating with stress levels experienced over extended periods.

14.9.5 Political Influence and Bureaucratic Processes (Stress/ Emotional Trauma)

The evolution of policies in this sector has been shaped by past failings and the lessons learned from them. In Australia, regardless of the jurisdiction, this environment is subject to both Federal and State Government oversight, encompassing numerous governmental departments. This heavy bureaucratic hand is mirrored in the private sector, with multiple departments overseeing counter-terrorism procedures.

Bureaucracies, regardless of sector, may try to influence policies for their own reasons, often disregarding hard-won insights. The situation worsens when these external entities try to alter these procedures without bearing any of the associated threat or risk. Such modifications can undermine operational capabilities, leading to increased workload, pressure, and stress, as well as fostering a feeling of betrayal among individuals.

14.9.6 Scrutiny (Stress)

Governments and communities generally expect every act of terrorism to be preventable. This assumption creates an unrealistic burden, shifting the responsibility of terrorism onto its professionals. Such reversed accountability results in disproportionate scrutiny of counter-terrorism professionals' actions and decisions by external entities that don't share the risk or operational responsibilities.

Overbearing scrutiny amplifies pressure and stress. To meet these demanding expectations and manage excessive oversight, professionals might work prolonged hours, exposing them to fatigue, burnout, and psychological harm.

14.9.7 Presence of the Dark Triad (Emotional Trauma)

The *dark triad* is a term used by psychologists to refer to three major personality disorders: psychopathy, Machiavellianism, and narcissism. These three disorders pose a threat to the psychological wellbeing of others.[70] The presence of these disorders is not only damaging to other people but may also be damaging to their organisation. Based on its nature and public profile, counter-terrorism seems to attract individuals who demonstrate the damaging characteristics of these personality disorders.

14.10 Common Pitfalls in Managing Personnel Suffering from Psychological Injuries

When dealing with personnel suffering from psychological injuries, organisations should aim to alleviate these injuries, facilitating the individual's recovery. Balancing the needs of the individual against those of the organisation is intricate and requires avoiding several common pitfalls.

14.10.1 False Assumption: Personnel Will Seek Support

One might expect that counter-terrorism professionals would seek support during times of psychological distress. However, research and experience suggest this is rarely the case. It's understood that seeking help is a personal decision, often influenced by the perceived organisational culture. If an organisation has a history of treating affected individuals poorly or displays bias against those seeking help, it can deter personnel from accessing support. There's a prevalent belief among these individuals that seeking psychological help might harm their career prospects.

14.10.2 Flexible Tailored Support

Large organisations often exhibit bureaucratic tendencies, especially regarding human resource management. This extends to how they handle personnel identified with psychological

---

[70] Erikson,T.

injuries, often resorting to a 'one size fits all' approach. Given the subjectivity of such injuries, support mechanisms should be flexible and tailored to the individual. This is a nuanced space, where a strategy that benefits one person might harm another.

14.10.3 Avoiding Triggers

Psychological injuries arise partly from experiences, exposure, and cognitive processes unique to the individual. Consequently, specific situations, conditions, individuals, sounds, or smells might provoke a response in the sufferer that exacerbates their condition. These provocations are termed as 'triggers'. Whenever possible, these triggers should be avoided.

14.10.4 Integrity of Support

Organisations may provide professional healthcare support to staff deemed vulnerable due to their employment domain. These initiatives are often termed 'well-check' programs. It's essential that support officers prioritise the individual over the organisation. If they are seen as acting on the organisation's behalf — extracting information for the organisation's advantage — the support process may become ineffective. Moreover, if an employee sustains a psychological injury at work, and it becomes a legal matter, the organisation must remain supportive and refrain from treating the individual as a potential litigant.

14.10.5 Family Links

Research shows that family members of sufferers also bear the brunt when stress and anxiety permeate the home. These family members can be seen as secondary sufferers, experiencing *indirect* or *vicarious trauma*. Few organisations offer family support, a neglect that not only shirks the organisation's duty of care to its employees and their families but can also further impact their workforce, especially if the sufferers' family members are employees. They too become vulnerable to psychological injuries through vicarious trauma.

14.10.6 'Lord Voldemort' Approach

Lord Voldemort, the chief antagonist in the 'Harry Potter' series, is notorious for a name that should not be spoken aloud, out of fear. In a parallel manner, organisations might inadvertently treat their psychologically injured staff as unmentionable. When a counter-terrorism expert succumbs to psychological injury, colleagues and superiors might avoid mentioning the person or their condition.

It's not to say this avoidance is malicious; it often arises from a lack of understanding or a deficient organisational culture. If a staff member sustains physical injuries in a terror event, they would typically receive visits, care, and support from colleagues. In contrast, if the injury were psychological, that same employee might find themselves navigating their recovery journey largely alone.

This approach can further isolate the individual. Their feelings of guilt, shame, anxiety, frustration, and anger might intensify due to this perceived neglect, possibly worsening their condition.

14.11 Summary

The counter-terrorism sector is inherently stressful, pressured, and traumatic, producing intense levels of anxiety. Chronic exposure to such anxiety can severely impact an individual's psychological wellbeing. The aim should be to protect counter-terrorism professionals by limiting their exposure to such toxic environments.

The widespread underestimation of these injuries' prevalence is inadvertently mirrored in both public and private organisations' cultures. Effective management of psychological health begins with self-monitoring and observing others, intervening when necessary. At the core of successful processes lies effective communication; managing psychological wellbeing is no exception.

While this guide champions psychological wellbeing, it also upholds the principle that only a qualified medical professional should diagnose and treat psychological injuries.

Everyone experiences psychological injuries differently. Recognising symptoms in counter-terrorism professionals is intricate. To aid, this book offers toolboxes highlighting potential indicators of psychological injuries. Early identification and timely intervention by medical professionals are paramount for the individual's psychological wellbeing.

Balancing the individual's needs against organisational requirements demands careful consideration, especially when navigating pitfalls like assumptions about seeking support, ensuring flexible and tailored assistance, steering clear of triggers, upholding the integrity of support, acknowledging the importance of family connections, and avoiding the 'Lord Voldemort' approach.

14.12 Key Points

- Counter-terrorism operates in a hostile environment, and prolonged exposure can adversely affect an individual's physical and psychological wellbeing.
- 'Psychological' is defined by Safe Work Australia as '...a range of cognitive, emotional and behavioural symptoms that interfere with a worker's life and can significantly affect how they feel, think behave and interact with others.'[71] It can occur after repeated and ongoing exposure to potentially traumatic events, loss and extreme stress.[72]
- This book adheres to the principle that only a qualified medical professional should diagnose and treat a psychological injury.
- Trauma is an emotional response to a significant event or situation that's physically or emotionally harmful,

---

[71] Safe Work Australia
[72] Papazoglou, K., Tuttle, B.

threatening, or makes an individual feel unsafe.[73] It can encompass a single event or a series of events over an extended period.

- Emotional trauma can be classed as either direct or indirect.
- Direct trauma refers to experiences directly undergone by the individual.
- Indirect trauma means the individual experiences trauma through others' accounts of traumatic events. This can be termed as vicarious trauma or secondary traumatic stress.
- Anxiety is an individual's behavioural response in anticipation to future events.
- Stress is considered to be the body's response to circumstances.
- Chronic exposure to stress can lead to emotional and mental exhaustion, commonly known as burnout.
- This book considers 'moral injury' as a direct emotional trauma that can contribute to or cause a psychological injury. From an organisational standpoint, such injury can stem from mismanagement, culture, poor leadership, and ill-advised decisions.

---

[73] American Psychological Association

Conclusion

Terrorism has evolved, expanding the responsibility for its counteraction beyond just law enforcement and security intelligence agencies to include all entities in the public and private sectors.

The prevailing principle now asserts that counter-terrorism is a shared responsibility of government and the community at large. This shift has effectively placed all organisations on the front line. Individuals within these organisations have transformed into counter-terrorism professionals in their respective expertise areas.

Counter-terrorism consists of a myriad of interconnected, ongoing processes. This book delves into several of these processes, framing them within the overarching 'counter-terrorism process' model. This process provides a structured approach for organisations to address terrorism threats. The goal is to optimize counter-terrorism efforts while reducing an organisation's risk exposure.

Effective decision-making in this realm is multifaceted. The success hinges on the consistent application of these concepts at every stage of the counter-terrorism process.

Drawing from hard-earned lessons in this challenging environment and extensive research, this book equips the next generation of counter-terrorism professionals and decision-makers with the essential principles and practical tools to proficiently address terrorism threats. The aspiration is that this book will enrich the expertise and skills of these professionals, enabling them to apply their knowledge in real-world scenarios, to prevent 'black swan' events such as the atrocities witnessed during the Hamas incursion into Israel in October 2023.

Lexicon

Many terms you will come across throughout this book will have different meanings in general conversation than when they are used in the context of counter-terrorism. To avoid misunderstandings, this book has adopted the following terms, definitions and naming conventions.

Anticipation: Anticipation is the process of looking forward to identify and evaluate the future state of a potential threat.

Actual Threat: In the context of this book, occurs when collection capabilities identify a person of interest/s (POI) who make a threat that would constitute a terrorism offence.

Belief: The term *belief* includes any religious, political or ideological convictions of an individual or group.

Collection Point: Includes every action of interaction by or with a person of interest that may potentially provide information of their intentions.

Convert: The term *convert* refers to a person who changes to, or is brought to embrace and profess, a particular belief.

Counter Radicalisation: Refers to an early intervention strategy, system or process, aimed at preventing or inhibiting radicalisation.

Counter-Terrorism Capabilities: Includes any discipline that collects information from the collection points via their unique operational methodologies.

Counter-Terrorism Professional: Includes individuals from either public or private sectors engaged in any form of counter terrorism activities

Decisions: *Decisions* are a cognitive process to determine and implement a course of action.

Deradicalisation: Refers to an intervention strategy, system or process, aimed at persuading a radicalised person or group to modify their belief system to the extent that they do not contravene Section 100.1 of the *Commonwealth Criminal Code Act* 1995 (Cth). [74]

Extremist: Refers to a person who passively supports the advancement of a political, religious or ideological cause through threats or actions of others, as defined in Section 100.1 of the *Commonwealth Criminal Code Act* 1995 (Cth).

Fundamentalism: The term *fundamentalist* refers to any individual that complies with the laws of that jurisdiction whilst holding a strict and literal adherence to a set of basic principles or adheres to a traditional form of belief.

Judgement: *Judgement* is defined as a cognitive measurement of an uncertainty which may apply objective or subjective processes, whose purpose is to form an opinion that supports a corresponding decision.

Management Continuum: The *Management Continuum* is the collective term for the perpetual treatment, management, mitigation and resolution strategies implemented to address an infinite terrorist threat.

Perceived Threat: In the context of this book, occurs when the collection capabilities identify circumstances, history or actions of POI/s that a reasonable person would find establishes a threat that would constitute a terrorism offence.

Radical: The term *radical* (or radicalised person) is someone who is prepared, directly or indirectly, to advance a political, religious or ideological cause through threats or actions as defined in Section 100.1 of the *Commonwealth Criminal Code Act* 1995 (Cth).

---

[74] Section 100.1 *Commonwealth Criminal Code Act 1995*. This legislation defines terrorism in Australia.

Reasonable Person: The *reasonable person test* is a legal term which has been defined as, 'a person who possess the faculty of reason and engages in conduct in accordance with community standards.'[75]

Revert: Refers to a convert who returns to their previous belief.

---

[75] Butt, P., Aitken, J.

Acronyms

ABDC	Australian Bomb Data Centre
ACAB	All Cops Are Bastards
ADF	Australian Defence Force
AGD	Attorney General's Department (Australian Government)
ACS	Australian Customs Service
AFP	Australian Federal Police
AIC	Australian Intelligence Community
ANSTO	Australian Nuclear Science & Technology Organisation
ANZCTC	Australian & New Zealand Counter Terrorism Committee
APM	Australian Police Medal
AQ	Al-Qa'ida
AQAP	Al Qa'ida in the Arabian Peninsula
AQIM	Al Qa'ida in the Islamic Maghreb
ARPC	Australian Reinsurance Pool Corporation
AS	Australian Standards
ASIO	Australian Security Intelligence Organisation
AUSTRAC	Australian Transaction Reports & Analysis Centre
BLM	Black Lives Matter
BOCSAR	NSW Bureau of Crime Statistics and Research
CBRN	Chemical, Biological, Radiological & Nuclear
CCTV	Closed-Circuit Television
CDO	Continuing Detention Order
CDPP	Commonwealth Director Public Prosecutions
CEO	Chief Executive Officer
CO	Control Order
COAG	Council of Australian Governments
COP	Commissioner of Police
COT	Cyber Operations Team

Cth	Commonwealth of Australia
CI	Critical Infrastructure
CVE	Countering Violent Extremism
DPP	Director Public Prosecutions (NSW)
DCS	Department of Corrective Services (NSW)
DA	Deliberate Action
DVI	Disaster Victim Identification
EA	Emergency Action
EMA	Emergency Management Australia
EQ	Emotional Quotient
ESO	Extended Supervision Order
ESP	Engagement & Support Panel
FOUO	For Official Use Only
GPO	General Post Office
HR	Human Resources
HRTO	High Risk Terrorism Offenders
HAZMAT	Hazardous Material
IAC	Intelligence Assessment Committee
ICCS	Integrated Control & Command System
ICO	Interim Control Order
IED	Improvised Explosive Device
INTREP	Intelligence Report
INTSUM	Intelligence Summary Report
IQ	Intelligence Quotient
IS	Islamic State
ISO	International Standards Organisation
JCTT	Joint Counter Terrorism Team
JeM	Jaish-e-Mohammed
JI	Jemaah Islamiyah
JIG	Joint Intelligence Group
KKK	Ku Klux Klan
LeT	Laskhar-e-Tayiba
LTTE	Liberation Tigers of Tamil Eelam
MOU	Memorandum of Understanding
NCTC	National Counter Terrorism Committee
NCTP	National Counter Terrorism Plan
NCTHB	National Counter Terrorism Handbook

NDA	National Disability Agreement
NDG	National Disruption Group
NDIS	National Disability Insurance Scheme
NGO	Non-Government Organisation
NIG	National Intelligence Group
NSH	National Security Hotline
NSI Act	National Security Information Act (Cth)
NSO	National Socialist Order
NSW	New South Wales
NSWPF	New South Wales Police Force
NTPOL	Northern Territory Police
NTS	National Terrorist Situation
NTAC	National Threat Assessment Centre
NZS	New Zealand Standards
PFC	Police Forward Commander
PFCP	Police Forward Command Post
PII	Public Interest Immunity
PIRA	Provisional Irish Republican Army
POI	Person of Interest
PMV	Politically Motivated Violence
PSPF	Protective Security Policy Framework
PTSD	Post-Traumatic Stress Disorder
QPOL	Queensland Police Service
RQ	Risk Quotient
SAC PAV	Standing Advisory Committee on Commonwealth /State Cooperation for Protection Against Violence
SAPOL	South Australian Police
SIO	Senior Investigating Officer
SITREP	Situation Report
SOP	Standard Operating Procedures
TA	Threat Assessment
TASPOL	Tasmanian Police
THRO	Terrorism High Risk Offender
ToR	Terms of Reference
TOU	Tactical Operations Unit
TPB	Theory of Planned Behaviour

UK	United Kingdom
USA	United States of America
USS	United States Ship
VICPOL	Victorian Police
VIP	Very Important Person
WAPOL	Western Australia Police
WH&S	Work, Health and Safety
XLW	Extreme Left Wing
XIM	Issue Motivated Extremism
XRW	Extreme Right Wing

Terrorist Organisations

In Australia, 29 organisations currently are officially proscribed as terrorist organisations in the *Criminal Code Regulations* (2002) (Cth). [76] As at 1 November 2023, these 29 organisations are: -

Abu Sayyaf Group	Philippines
Al Qa'ida (Al Qaeda)	Global
Al Qa'ida in Arabian Peninsula (AQAP)	Yemen
Al Qa'ida in the Indian Subcontinent (AQIS)	India
Al Qa'ida in the Islamic Maghreb (AQIM)	Algeria
Al Shabaab	Somalia
Boko Haram	Nigeria (West Africa)
Hamas's Izz Din al-Qassam Brigades	Palestine
Hay'at tahrir al-sham	Syria
Hizballah External Security Organisation	Lebanon
Hurras al_Din	Syria
Islamic State (IS)	Iraq/Syria/ Global
Islamic State East Asia	East Asia
Islamic State in Libya (IS-Libya)	Libya
Islamic State Khorasan Province	Pakistan
Islamic State Sinai Province (IS-Sinai)	Sinai
Islamic State Somalia	Somalia
Islamic State West Africa Province	Nigeria
Jaish-e-Mohammed (JeM)	Pakistan
Jama'at Mujahideen Bangladesh	Banglasdesh
Jama'at Nusrat al-Islam wal-Muslim	Lebanon
Jemaah Islamiyah (JI)	Indonesia
Kurdistan Workers Party (PKK)	Turkey

---

[76] Criminal Code Regulations 2002 (Commonwealth)

Laskhar –e- Tayiba (LeT)	Pakistan
National Socialist Order (NSO)	USA
Neo-Jama'at Mujahideen	Bangladesh
Palestinian Islamic Jihad	Palestine
Sonnenkrieg Division	UK
The Base	USA

This list is maintained by the Attorney General's Department, Australian Government and any updates can be located by following the link: https://www.ag.gov.au/national-security/ australias-counter-terrorism-laws/terrorist-organisations

List of Case Studies

List of Tool Boxes

Lexicon (Radicalisation) Tool Box

Lexicon (Belief) Tool Box

Characteristics (XRW) Tool Box

Characteristics (XLW) Tool Box

Characteristics (XSI) Tool Box

Characteristics (Generational Radicalisation) Tool Box

Characteristics (Cognitive Opening Radicalisation) Tool Box

Characteristics (Fixated Radicalisation) Tool Box

Characteristics (Mental Health Radicalisation) Tool Box

Characteristics (Extrinsic Radicalisation) Tool Box

Indicators (Generational Radicalisation) Tool Box

Indicators (Cognitive Opening Radicalisation) Tool Box

Indicators (Fixated Radicalisation) Tool Box

Indicators (Mental Health Radicalisation) Tool Box

Indicators (Extrinsic Radicalisation) Tool Box

Common Causes Implementation Gaps Tool Box

Behavioural / Physical Indicators (Potential Psychological Injuries) Tool Box

Emotional / Cognitive Indicators (Potential Psychological Injuries) Tool Box

Australian Terrorism Calendar Tool Box

ANNEXURE 1

AUSTRALIAN TERRORISM CALENDAR TOOLBOX

Date	Year	January Incident
1	1915	Australia: Two gunmen of Turkish origin attacked a picnic train in Broken Hill; six people died, including the two gunmen.
	1964	The Palestinian Liberation Organisation (PLO) was founded.
	2017	Australia: JCTT Operation San Jose arrested Ali Khalif Shire Ali for planning a terrorist attack in Federation Square, Melbourne.
2		
3		
4		
5		
6	1963	The Colombian National Liberation Army (ELN) was founded.
	2021	USA: Washington Capitol Riots.
7		
	2015	France: The Kouachi brothers attacked *Charlie Hebdo Magazine* in Paris, killing 11 people.
8	1998	USA: Ramzi Ahmed Yousef was sentenced to life plus 240 years for the 1993 World Trade Centre bombings.
9		
10		
11		
12		
13		
14		
15	1989	Australia: Arson attack on a Chinese restaurant in Perth.
16	1971	Australia: Bombing of the Soviet Embassy in Canberra.
	1996	USA: Sentencing of Umar Abd al-Rahman (the Blind Shiekh) to life for the 1993 bombing of the World Trade Centre.

	1991	Iraq: US-led coalition military operation, Desert Storm, commenced.
17		
18		
19	1987	Australia: Bombing of Roma Street Mail Exchange in Brisbane.
	1989	Australia: Arson attack on a Chinese restaurant in Perth.
20		
21		
22	2017	Australia: Vehicle attack on Bourke Street Mall, Melbourne.
23		
24	1973	Australia: A letter bomb was sent to the Jewish community in Sydney (Black September).
25		
	1991	Australia: A man was arrested for attempting to hijack a plane in Sydney.
	2016	Australia: JCTT Operation Chillon arrested Sameh Bayda and Alo-Bridget Namoa (referred to as the 'Islamic Bonnie and Clyde')[79] for conspiring to plan a terrorist attack in Sydney.
27		
28	1989	Australia: Drive-by shooting of the residence of a member of the African National Congress in Sydney (XRW).
29		
30		
31		

---

[77] ABC News

Date	Year	February Incident
1	2004	Australia: Arson attacks on three Chinese restaurants in Perth.
2	2017	Australia: Operation Marksburg arrested Haisem Zahab for providing support to the terrorist organisation Islamic State, Young, NSW.
3		
4		
5		
6	2004	Russia: Bombing of Moscow Metro, killing 40 people and injuring 122.
7		
8	1979	Australia: Authorities uncovered a terrorist plot by Yugoslav targets to poison Sydney Water.
9	2018	Australia: JCTT Operation Vecchio, a female was arrested for stabbing her landlord in Mill Park, Victoria, inspired by IS.
10	2015	Australia: JCTT Operation Castrum arrested Kaid and Al-Kuobi for preparing to commit a terrorist attack on behalf of Islamic State, Fairfield, Sydney.
11		
12		
13	1978	Australia: Hilton bombing, killing three people and injuring 6, Sydney (Ananda Marga).
14	1972	Australia: Armed attack on Yugoslav Consulate in Perth.
15	1999	Turkey: Arrest of PKK leader Ocalan in Nairobi; returned to Turkey for trial.
16	1972	Australia: Bombing of Yugoslav travel agency in Sydney.
17		
18		
19	2001	UK: Enactment of the UK Terrorism Act 2000.
20	1991	Australia: Arson attack on the American/Australian Association in Sydney.

21		
22	**1969**	Palestine: Democratic Front for the Liberation of Palestine was founded.
23		
24	**1998**	Afghanistan: Osama Bin Laden and Al Qaeda issued a fatwa against the USA.
	2022	Russia began its full invasion of the Ukraine.
25		
26		
	1993	USA: Bombing of the World Trade Centre, killing 6 people and injuring 1000.
27		
28		

Date	Year	March Incident
1	**2000**	New Zealand: Authorities in New Zealand located plans for a terrorist attack on ANSTO, Sydney.
	2003	Pakistan: Khalid Shaykh Muhammad (KSM) arrested for his role in 9/11 attacks (AQ).
2		
3		
4		
5	**1804**	Australia: Battle at Castle Hill, where 230 convicts staged an uprising, resulting in the deaths of 15 convicts and a further 9 being executed.
6		
7		
8		
9		
10		
11	**2004**	Spain: Abu Hafs al-Masri Brigade claimed responsibility for the bomb attacks on Spanish trains, killing 198 people and injuring 600.
12		
13		
14	**1994**	Australia: Bombing of the Greek Australian Organisation in Melbourne.
15	**2019**	New Zealand: Christchurch shootings at the Al Noor Mosque and Linwood Islamic Centre, killing 51 people and injuring 40. (XRW attack). The offender - Brenton Tarrant from NSW.
16		
17	**2021**	Australia: JCTT Operation Loonbeek, three males were arrested for terrorist activity in Victoria.
18		
19	**1932**	Australia: Francis de Groot, member of the New Guard, cut the ribbon for the Sydney Harbour Bridge opening.

	1995	Japan: Sarin gas attack on Tokyo rail system, killing 12 people and injuring 5000 (Aum Shinrikyo).
20	**2020**	Australia: JCTT Operation Templeogue, POIs of interest arrested for planning to conduct a terrorist attack in Nowra, NSW (XRW).
21		
22	**1998**	Australia: Arson attack on residence for the South African Embassy employee.
	1945	Arab League was founded.
23		
24	**2006**	Australia: JCTT Operation Cheer; a couple was arrested for planning to bomb Kings Cross, Sydney.
25	**1978**	Australia: Bomb detected and defused at Indian High Commission residence in Canberra.
	1994	Australia: Attack on German Consulate in Melbourne.
26		
27		
28		
29		
30		
31		

Date	Year	April Incident
1	1970	El Salvador: Popular Forces of Liberation was founded.
2	1986	Greece: Bombing of TWA flight 840, killing four people and injuring nine.
3		
4	1979	Australia: Attempted hijacking of Pan Am flight at Sydney airport. Offender shot and killed by police.
5		
6	1992	Australia: Armed intrusion at the Iranian Embassy in Canberra.
7	2017	Australia: Two young males robbed a service station in Queanbeyan, killing the attendant and writing 'IS' on the service station window.
8		
9		
10		
11	1968	Palestine: Popular Front for the Liberation of Palestine – General Command was founded.
12		
13		
14		
15	2004	Australia: JCTT Operation Newport arrested a medical student training with a terrorist organisation in Pakistan. Prosecution ceased.
	2013	USA: Bombing at the Boston Marathon, killing three people and injuring 280.
16		
17		
18	1991	Australia: Assassination of Dr Morcos in Sydney (anti-Islamic stance).
	2015	Australia: JCTT Operation Rising, three offenders arrested for planning a terrorist attack in Melbourne.
19	1993	USA: WACO siege in Texas resulted in the deaths of 76 people.

	1995	USA: Bombing of the Alfred P. Murrah Federal Building in Oklahoma City, killing 168 people.
	1972	Australia: Bombing of the Australian Communist Office in Brisbane
20	**1889**	Austria: Adolf Hitler was born.
21	**1991**	Australia: National Action member, Perry Whitehouse, killed fellow member Wayne Smith in Tempe, Sydney.
22	**2004**	Australia: JCTT Operation Newport arrested Lodhi for planning a terrorist attack.
23		
24	**1979**	Australia: Letter bomb was sent to a department store in Perth.
	2016	Australia: JCTT Operation Vianden arrested a young person for planning a terrorist attack in Sydney.
25		Australia: ANZAC DAY.
26	**1972**	Australia: Bombing of the residence of a pro-Yugoslav political figure.
27		
28	**2016**	Australia: JCTT Operation Appleby arrested ATAI for planning a terrorist attack in Sydney.
29		
30		

Date	Year	May Incident
1	**1985**	Australia: Bombing of the Melbourne Coroners Court.
	2007	Australia: Arrest of LTTE members in Western Sydney and Melbourne.
2	**2006**	USA: Zacarias Moussaoui was sentenced to life imprisonment for his role in the 9/11 terrorist attacks.
	2011	Pakistan: Killing of Osama Bin Laden by US Special Forces, Operation Neptune's Spear.
3	**2014**	Australia: JCTT Operation Duntulm, Elomar arrested for supporting foreign fighters at Sydney Airport.
4		
5		
6		
7		
8	**2015**	Australia: JCTT Operation Amberd arrested a male for planning a terrorist attack in Melbourne.
9		
10		
11	**2016**	Australia: JCTT Operation Middleham arrested offenders in northern Queensland for attempting to leave Australia via boat to fight in Syria ('Tinnie Terrorists').
12		
13		
14	**1948**	Israel: State of Israel was founded.
15	**1948**	Palestine: Nakba Day was founded – Recognising the displacement of Palestinians from their homeland by Israel.
16		
17	**2016**	Australia: JCTT Operation Sanadres arrested Khaja for planning a terrorist attack in Sydney.

18	1978	Australia: Bombing of the NSW Police Headquarters.
	2009	Sri Lanka: Death of Prabhakaran, leader of LTTE.
19		
20	2002	East Timor: Independence Day.
21		
22		
23		
24	2000	Lebanon: Israeli troops withdrew from Lebanon after 22 years of occupation.
25	1975	Australia: Bombing on Sunny Adriatic Trade & Tourist Centre (Yugoslav), Melbourne.
	2020	USA: George Floyd killed in Minneapolis by Police (BLM).
26	2016	Australia: JCTT Operation arrested Said for attempting to conduct a terrorist attack in Sydney.
27	1978	Australia: Bombing of the residence of the Indian Ambassador in Sydney.
	1990	The Netherlands: PIRA killed two innocent Australians, mistaking them for being off-duty members of the UK armed forces.
28		
29		
30		
31		

Date	Year	June Incident
1		
2	2004	Australia: JCTT operation arrested Khazaal for terrorist offences in Sydney.
	2006	Canada: Counter-terrorism operation led to the arrest of 17 offenders for planning a terrorist attack.
3		
4		
5	2017	Australia: Terrorist attack in Brighton, Melbourne, where Yaqub Khayre killed one person, and was killed by Police.
6		
7		
8		
9		
10		
11		
12		
13		
14	2016	Australia: JCTT Operation Himeji arrested a young person in Sydney for planning a terrorist attack. Charges later withdrawn and the young person managed under mental health protocols.
	2017	Australia: Strike Force Murramah in Sydney arrested a male for attempting to stab a police officer, religion-inspired.
15	1985	Australia: Bombing of the NSW Nurses Association in Sydney.
16		
17	1995	Australia: Arson attack on the French Consulate in Perth.
18		
19		
20		

21	**1966**	Australia: Attempted assassination of Federal Opposition Leader Calwell in Mosman, Sydney.
22		
23		
24		
25		
26		
27		
28	**1993**	Australia: Intrusion of United Nations Offices, Sydney by pro- Kurdistan supporters.
29		
30		

Date	Year	July Incident
1	2019	Australia: JCTT Operation Zellaer arrested and charged as an offender for attempting to conduct a terrorist attack in Sydney.
2	2007	Australia: JCTT operation led to the arrest of Dr. Haneef in Brisbane due to alleged links to terrorism. Charges were later withdrawn; Dr. Haneef was found innocent of all allegations.
3		
4		
5	1985	Australia: Bombing at the Union Carbide building in Sydney.
6		
7	2005	UK: Synchronised bombings of the London transport system, known as the 7/7 bombings.
8		
9		
10		
11	2006	India: Synchronised attacks in Mumbai by members of LeT killed up to 200 people and injured 900 others.
12	2016	Australia: JCTT operation led to the arrest of Al Qudsi, who was charged with offences relating to foreign incursion for the Syrian conflict.
13	1985	Australia: Drive-by shooting at the Vietnamese Consulate in Sydney.
14	2008	Australia: Santhirarajah, a member of the LTTE, was deported from Australia to the USA on terrorism charges.
	2016	France: A terrorist used a prime mover to kill 86 people in Nice during France's Independence Day celebrations.
	2016	Australia: JCTT operation led to the arrest of Abdirahman for being a member of the Islamic State.
15		

16	**2001**	Australia: Shooting at the East Melbourne Fertility Clinic
17	**2002**	Greece: The founder of the November 17 terrorist group, Alexandros Yiotopoulos, was arrested.
18	**2014**	Australia: JCTT Operation Appleby led to the arrest of Al-Talebi for planning a terrorist attack.
19		
20		
21	**1970**	Australia: Bombing at the Yugoslav Consulate in Melbourne.
22	**2011**	Norway: Breivik conducted a terrorist attack in Oslo and Utoya Island, killing 77 people.
23		
24		
25		
26		
27		
28		
29	**2017**	Australia: JCTT Operation Silves resulted in the arrest of multiple offenders involved in a plot to bomb a commercial airline.
30		
31		

Date	Year	August *Incident*
1		
2	**1990**	Kuwait: Iraq invaded Kuwait.
3	**1996**	Australia: Bombing at the Australian Government Offices in Coffs Harbour, NSW.
4	**2009**	Australia: JCTT Operation Neath led to the arrest of five offenders planning a terrorist attack on the Holsworthy Military Base.
5		
6	**2005**	Australia: JCTT Operation Restormel resulted in the arrest of two young people planning a terrorist attack in Sydney.
	2016	Australia: JCTT Operation Fortaleza in Melbourne led to the arrest of a male planning a terrorist attack.
7		
8		
9		
10		
11		
12		
13		
14		
15		
16		
17		
18		
19		
20		
21		
22		
23		
24		

25		
26		
27		
28		
29	**1977**	Australia: Arson attack on the Indian High Commission in Canberra.
30		
31	**1977**	Australia: Arson attack on the Australian Atomic Energy Commission.

Date	Year	September Incident
1	**1970**	Jordan: Palestinian guerrillas were expelled from Jordan. The terrorist group adopted the name 'Black September'.
	1972	Australia: Five letter bombs sent by the terrorist group, Black September, to various locations.
	1988	Australia: Two arson attacks on Chinese restaurants in Perth.
	1989	Australia: Two members of the Australian National Movement tortured and killed a fellow member for being a suspected informant.
	2004	Russia: Terrorist attack on the Beslan School, resulting in the deaths of 330 people and injuring 776 others, orchestrated by Chechen separatists.
2		
3	**1854**	Australia: Eureka Stockade raided by authorities resulting in the deaths 27 miners and 5 soldiers – (Noted not an act of terrorism).
4		
5	**1972**	Germany: Terrorist attack on the Munich Olympic Games by members of Black September.
	1994	Australia: Assassination of NSW Politician John Newman in Cabramatta, Sydney. Phuong Ngo was convicted.
6		
7		
8		
9		
	2001	Afghanistan: Ahmad Masood, the leader of the Northern Alliance, was assassinated by members of Al Qaeda.
	2004	Indonesia: Terrorist attack on the Australian Embassy in Jakarta killed 10 and injured 150.
10	**2014**	Australia: JCTT Operation Bolton resulted in the arrest of Kruezi for planning a terrorist attack.

	2016	Australia: In JCTT Operation Tressider, Khan was arrested in Minto, South Western Sydney, for conducting a terrorist attack.
11	**2001**	USA: Al Qaeda orchestrated multiple attacks, known as 9/11, killing approximately 3,000 people initially.
12	**1991**	Australia: Shooting at the Indonesian Consulate in Darwin.
13		
14		
	2016	Australia: JCTT Operation Broughton led to charges against Hraiche for terrorism offences in NSW.
15	**1977**	Australia: The Indian Defence attaché and his wife were kidnapped in Canberra; the attaché was stabbed.
16		
17		
18	**2014**	Australia: JCTT Operation Appleby led to the arrest of Azari, who was planning a terrorist attack.
19	**1985**	Australia: Bombing at the Canterbury Race Meeting targeting horses.
20	**1984**	Lebanon: The Islamic Jihad bombed the US Embassy in Beirut, killing 23 people.
21		
22	**2014**	Syria: Al Adnani, the Emir of the Islamic State, issued a fatwa to attack the West.
23	**2014**	Australia: A terrorist attacked two JCTT members at the Endeavour Hills Police Station in Victoria. The offender, Numan Haider, was shot and killed by the police.
24		
25	**1916**	Murder of Constable Duncan in Tottenham, NSW by the Wobblies. (Australia's first police officer killed on duty through terrorism)
26		
27		
28		
29		
30		

Date	Year	October Incident
1	1972	Australia: Two letter bombs were sent to various members of the Australian Jewish community (Black September).
	2005	Bali: A terrorist attack in Bali (Bali 2) resulted in a bombing that killed 26 people (Jemaah Islamiyah).
2	2015	Australia: A terrorist attack at the NSW Police Headquarters killed Curtis Cheng in Parramatta; authorities killed the offender.
3		
4		
5		
6	1973	Israel: The Yom Kippur War began.
	1981	Egypt: President Sadat assassinated by Egyptian Islamic Jihad.
7	2001	Afghanistan: US-led coalition began military offensive in Afghanistan in response to 9/11 attacks.
7	2023	Israel: Terrorist attack, Hamas Incursion into Israel killing over 1300 innocent civilians.
8		
9		
10	1993	Norway: Assailants shot the Norwegian publisher of 'The Satanic Verses' three times.
11		
12	2000	Yemen: Terrorist attack and bombing of USS *Cole*, killing 17 people (Al Qaeda).
	2002	Bali: Terrorist attack (Bali 1) involving multiple bombs explode in the night club district of Kuta, killing 202 people (Jemaah Islamiyah).
	2016	Australia: JCTT Operation Restormel resulted in the arrest of two young males for planning a terrorist attack in Sydney.
13		
14		

216

15	**2015**	Australia: JCTT Operation Peqin-Fellows resulted in the arrest of Alou with planning a terrorist attack in Sydney.
	1991	Australia: Arson attack on the residence of a pro-Croatian figure in Melbourne.
16	**1975**	East Timor: Four Australian journalists were killed in Baibo by Indonesian irregular troops.
17		
18		
19	**1977**	Australia: Terrorists attacked a member of Air India in Melbourne.
20		
21	**2014**	Canada: Terrorists attacked two soldiers near Ottawa by driving a vehicle into them. Attack inspired by Islamic State.
22	**2014**	Canada: Terrorist attack involving a lone gunman in Parliament Hill, Ottawa, inspired by Islamic State
23	**1983**	Lebanon: Islamic Jihad bombed US Marine and French barracks in Beirut, killing 24 Marines and 58 French paratroopers.
	2014	USA: A man inspired by the Islamic State attacked two New York Policemen with an axe.
24		
25		
26		
27		
28		
29		
30		
31	**1984**	India: Terrorist attack resulted in the assassination of Indian Prime Minister Indira Gandhi.

Date	Year	November Incident
1		
2	1972	Australia: A letter bomb was sent to a member of the Jewish community (Black September).
	1978	Cambodia: Australian yachtsmen were captured by the Khmer Rouge and later executed.
3	2016	Australia: Under JCTT Operation Bieber, individuals were arrested in Sydney for foreign incursion offences.
4	1979	Iran: Protesters seized the US Embassy in Tehran, taking 66 hostages.
5		
6	1980	Australia: A bombing occurred at the Iwasaki Resort, Queensland.
7		
9	2005	Australia: Under JCTT Operation Pendennis (Eden), 21 offenders were arrested in Sydney and Melbourne for various terrorist offences.
9	2018	Australia: In Operation Craggenburg, a male set a car on fire on Bourke Street, Melbourne, and stabbed three people, killing one. The offender was shot and killed by the police.
10		
11		
12	1983	Australia: A bomb was found at ANSTO, Sydney.
13	1978	Australia: Six people linked to the Assyrians Universal Alliance were hospitalized after being poisoned in Fairfield, NSW.
	2015	France: Coordinated terrorist attacks in Paris killed 130 people.
14		
15		
16		
	2016	Australia: JCTT operation, offender was charged in Sydney for foreign incursion offences.

17	**1966**	Australia: A parcel bomb exploded at the Melbourne GPO.
18	**2002**	Australia: Jack Roche was arrested for planning a terrorist attack on the Israeli Embassy.
19	**1975**	Australia: A letter bomb sent to the Queensland Premier injured a staff member.
20	**2018**	Australia: Under JCTT Operation Donabate, offenders planning a terrorist attack in Melbourne were arrested.
21	**1988**	Australia: An arson attack targeted a Chinese Restaurant in Perth.
22		
23	**1971**	Australia: The Yugoslav Trade Agency in Australia was bombed.
	1986	Australia: A bombing at the Turkish Consulate in Melbourne killed one of the bombers.
24		
25		
26		
27	**1988**	Australia: A Croatian youth was shot while demonstrating outside the Yugoslav Consulate in Sydney.
	2017	Australia: Under JCTT Operation San Jose, a male was arrested in Melbourne for planning a NYE terrorist attack.
	2020	Australia: Under JCTT Operation Queensland, a male was charged with terrorism offences.
28	**2021**	Australia: A male was arrested after a siege in Windang, NSW.
29		
30		

Date	Year	December Incident
1		
2		
3	**1977**	Australia: The Yuglosav Airlines office was bombed.
	2003	Australia: NSW Police arrested Mallah in Sydney, the first person charged under new Australian counter-terrorism legislation (found not guilty of terrorism offences at trial).
4	**2014**	Australia: Under JCTT Operation Holessalzburg, El Sabsabi was arrested in Melbourne for foreign incursion offences.
5		
6		
7	**1975**	East Timor: An Australian journalist was killed in Dili while investigating the murders of the Balibo 4.
8		
9	**2020**	Australia: Under a JCTT Operation, a male was arrested for planning a terrorist attack (XRW).
10	**2015**	Australia: Under JCTT Operation, five offenders were arrested in Sydney for planning a terrorist attack.
11	**2016**	Australia: Three offenders inspired by the Islamic State conducted an arson attack on a Shia Mosque in Melbourne.
12	**2005**	Australia: The Cronulla riots took place.
	2022	Australia: In Wieambilla, QLD, three offenders ambushed and shot two police officers and one civilian. The police shot and killed the offenders, who were inspired by an extreme belief.
13		
14		
15	**2014**	Australia: A lone gunman took hostages at the Lindt Café in Sydney; police killed the gunman, two innocent victims were also killed.
	2014	Australia: Under JCTT Operation Appleby, Al Talebi was arrested for terrorism funding.

16		
17	**1980**	Australia: The Turkish Consul-General and his bodyguard were assassinated in Dover Heights, Sydney.
	2020	Australia: In Brisbane, a male killed an elderly couple and was subsequently shot and killed by the police. The attack was religiously inspired.
18	**2014**	Australia: Under JCTT Operation Appleby, Sulayman was arrested in Sydney for terrorism offences.
19	**1971**	Australia: The Hub Theatre in Newtown, Sydney, was bombed.
20		
21	**1988**	Scotland: Pan Am Flight 103 was bombed over Lockerbie, killing 259 people.
	2017	Australia: In Melbourne, Noori drove his car into pedestrians on Flinders Street.
	2016	Australia: Under JCTT Operation Kastelholm, five offenders were arrested in Melbourne's CBD for planning a terrorist attack.
22	**2016**	Australia: Under a JCTT Operation, El Mir was arrested in Sydney for foreign incursion offences.
23	**1982**	Australia: Two bombings occurred in Sydney, targeting the Israeli Consulate and the Hakoah Club (Cold Case Investigation Forbearance).
	2016	Australia: Under JCTT Operation Kastlehom, four offenders were arrested in Melbourne for planning a terrorist attack.
24		
25		
26		
27		
28		
29		
30		

References

Acronym (1971). *The Concise Oxford Dictionary.* Oxford University Press.

Apgar, D. (2006). *Risk Intelligence: Learning to Manage What We Don't Known.* Harvard Business School Press, Boston, Massachusetts.

Australian Government (2002). Criminal Code Regulations.

Australian Government (2010). *Australian Government White Paper Terrorism 2010.* Canberra.

Australian Government (2022). *The Terrorism Pool.* The Australian Reinsurance Pool Corporation.

Bandura, A. (1971). *Social Learning Theory.* General Learning Press, New York.

Barnes, M. (2017). *Inquest into deaths arising from Lindt cafe seige: findings and recommendations.* State Coroner NSW, Sydney.

Beutell, N., O'Hare, M., Scheer, J., & Alset, J. (2017). Coping with Fear of an Exposure to Terrorism among Expatriates. *International Journal of Envrionment Research and Public Health.*

Butt, P., & Aitken, J. (2004). *Peisse – The Elements of Drafting.* Law Book Co, Sydney.

Campos, A. Vivacqua, A. Borges, M. (2010). *Supporting the Decision Implementation Process.* G.Kolschoten, T.Hermann, & S.Lukosch (Eds) CRIWG 2010 LNCS 6257, pp113-120.

Clun, R. (2022, October 16). *'The $60 billion question: how to fund and run the NDIS.'* The Sydney Morning Herald.

Cook, T. (2019). *Blackstones Senior Investigating Officers' Handbook.* Oxford University Press, Oxford.

Crenshaw, M. (1981). The Causes of Terrorism. *Comparative Politics,* 13(4), 385.

Dawson, L. (2009). 'The study of New Religious Movements and the Radicalisation of Home-Grown Terrorists: Opening a Dialogue.' *Terrorism and Political Violence,* 22(1), 1-21.

Dillon, H. (2019). *A Probe in the System: Medical Inquests in NSW.* Precedent AULA, 4.

Emotional Trauma. (2022). *American Psychological Association.*

Evans, D. (2012). *Risk Intelligence How to Live With Uncertainty.* Free Press, New York.

Erikson, T. (2022). *Surrounded by Narcissists.* Penguin Random House UK.

Gagne, E. D., Yekovich, C.W., & Yekovich, F.R. (1993). *The Cognitive Psychology of School Learning.* Harper Collins, New York.

Gawel, D. (2013). *Anticipating the Unknowns: An Australian Terrorism Investigations Strategy.* Doctor of Policing Thesis, Charles Sturt University.

Griffin, R. (2022). *What is Vertical Communication? Advantages and Disadvantages of Vertical Communications.* Retrieved from https://the businesscommunication.com/vertical-communication-advantages-and-disadvantages.

Guardian (2017, June 6). *Yacub Khayre Melbourne siege gunman's history of violence and drugs.* Retreieved from https://www.theguardian.com/australia-news/2017/jun/06/yacqub-khayre-melbourne-siege-gunmans-history-of-violent-and-drugs.

Henderson, P. (2005). *Frank Browne and the Neo-Nazis.* Labour History, 73–86.

Henfrey, N. (2021, December 12). George Santayana. *Encycolopedia Britannica.* Retreived from https://www.britannica.com/biography/George-Santayana.

Hoffman, B. (2006). *Inside Terrorism.* Columbia University Press, New York.

Jackson, B., Baker, J., Cragin, K., Parachini, J., Trujillo, H., Chalk, P. (2005). Aptitude for Destruction Volume 1: *Organisational Learning in Terrorist Groups and its Implications for Combating Terrorism.* The RAND Corporation.

Jamieson, N. (2020). Military Moral Injury: A Concept Analysis. *International Journal of Mental Health Nursing,* 29, 1049–1066.

Janis, I. L. (1972). *Victims of groupthink: A psychological study of foreign-policy decisions and fiascoes.* Houghton Mifflin.

Janis, I. L., Mann, L. (1977). *Decision making: A psychological analysis of conflict, choice, and committment.* Free Press, New York.

Jinkerson, J. (2016). Defining and assessing moral injury: A syndrome perspective. *Traumatology: An International Journal, 22,* 122–130.

Jinkerson, J., & Batlles, A.R. (2019). Relationships between moral injury syndrome model variables in combat veterans. *Traumatology: An International Journal,* 25, 33–40.

Kahneman, D. (2013). *Thinking Fast and Slow.* Farrar, Straus & Giroux.

Kahneman, D,. Sibony, O., Sunstein, C.R. (2021). *Noise: A flaw in human judgement.* William Collins, London.

Knight, C. (2019). Instrumental red teaming of 'terrorism': attack-concept gaming to develop comprehensive, anticipation, and resilence. *Journal of Criminological Research, Policy and Practice,* 93–94.

Leson, J. (2003). *Assessing and Managing the Terrorist Threat.* Bureau of Justice, Department of Justice USA.

Lini, S., Favier, P.A., Serantie, X., Vallerpir, B., & Hourlier, S. (2011). Developing ASAP (Anticipation Support for Aeronautical Planning). *16th International Symposium on Aviation Psychology,* (627–632). Dayton, OH.

Litz, B. T., Stein, N., Delaney, E., et al. (2009). Moral injury and moral repair in war veterans: A preliminary model and intervention strategy. *Clinical Psychology Review,* 29, 695–706.

Mellis, C. (2007). *Amsterdam & Radicalisation: The Municipal Approach.* The Hague: NCTB Radicalisation in broader perspective.

Motivation, E. (2010). *International Encylopedia of Education (3rd Ed).*

NDIS (2023, April 27). *Albanese Government invests in fighting fraud against NDIS.* Media release from the Minister.

Neumann, P. (2010) *Prisons & Terrorism: Radicalisation and De-radicalisation in 15 countries.* London: International Centre for the Study of Radicalisation and Political Violence (July).

Papazoglou, K. Tuttle, B. (2018) *Fighting Police Trauma: Practical Approaches for Addressing Psychological Needs of Officers.* Journal of Police Emergency Response.

Pickering, S. Wright-Neville, D. McCulloch, J. & Lentini, P. (2007) *Counter-Terrorism Policy & Culturally Diverse Communities Final Report.* Monash University.

Parliament of Australia (2018). *The National Disability Insurance Scheme: a chronology.*

Pike, B.(2022) *Ex-ADF Boss Sir Peter Cosgrove responds to the Defence and Veteran Suicide Royal Commission Report.* Daily Telegraph newspaper (14/8/2022).

Pruncken, H. (2010) *Handbook of Scientific Methods of Inquiry for Intelligence Analysis.* Scarecrow Press.

Oxford University Press (2022) *Concise Oxford Dictionary.*

O'Reilly, J. (2007) Detective Superintendent (ret) Counter Terrorism Command NSW Police Force.

Rapoport, D. (2004) *The Four Waves of Modern Terrorism.* A.K Cronin, J.M Ludes (Eds) Attacking Terrorism: Elements of a Grand Strategy (pp.46-73) Georgetown University Press.

Royal Commission into Defence and Veteran Suicide (2022) *Interim Report.* Commonwealth of Australia.

Shay, J. (1995) *Achillies in Vietnam: combat Trauma and the Undoing of Character.* Simon & Schuster.

Standards Australia (2009) *Risk Management – Principles and Guidelines (ISO 13000)*

Tryfos, P. (2001) *Chapter 3 Decision Theory*

Tusikou, N. Fahlamn, R. (2008) *Threat & Risk Assessments. Radcliff (Ed)* Strategic Thinking in Criminal Intelligence.

Victorian Police (2022). The Victorian Police Counter-Terrorism Strategy 2022–2025. Appendix B – Timeline of Major Terrorist Incidents in Australia since 2005.

Wiktorowicz, Q. (2005) *Radical Inslam Rising: Muslim Extremism in the West.* Rowman & Littlefield Publishers.

Zammit, A. (2012) *The Holswothy Barracks Plot: A case Study of an Al-Shabab Support Network in Australia.* Comabting Terrorism Centre, Volume 5, Issue 6.

www.ingramcontent.com/pod-product-compliance
Lightning Source LLC
Chambersburg PA
CBHW052111030426
42335CB00025B/2929